The
Iguana

An Owner's Guide To

A HAPPY HEALTHY PET

Howell Book House

Howell Book House
A Simon & Schuster Macmillan Company
1633 Broadway
New York, NY 10019

Library of Congress Cataloging-in-Publication Data
Rosenthal, Karen.
The iguana : an owner's guide to a happy healthy pet / by Karen Rosenthal.
p. cm.
ISBN 0-87605-478-5
1. Iguanas as pets.   I. Title.
SF459.I38R67   1996
639.3'95—dc20   96-20450
                                         CIP

Manufactured in the United States of America
10 9 8 7 6 5 4 3 2

Series Director: Dominique De Vito
Series Assistant Director: Ariel Cannon
Book Design: Michele Laseau
Cover Design: Iris Jeromnimon
Illustration: Jeff Yesh

front cover, top: Scott McKiernan/Zuma Press
  bottom: Mary Bloom
Joan Balzarini: 68, 105
Davis Barber: 9, 34, 57, 104, 106
Mary Bloom: 6, 73
Paulette Braun/Pets by Paulette: 18, 28, 33, 56, 97
Anthony Delprete: 40–41, 72, 96, 98, 101, 102, 103
Bob Klein: 22
Scott McKiernan/Zuma Press: 11, 30
Michael Siino: 10, 17, 48, 70, 76, 80
Jerry Williams: 5, 7, 8, 12, 15, 19, 24, 25, 27, 31, 35, 36, 38, 42, 43, 45, 46, 47, 50, 51,
    54, 60, 61, 62, 63, 65, 66, 69, 77, 81, 82, 85, 88, 99, 100, 108

Production Team: Trudy Brown, Jama Carter, Kathleen Caulfield, Trudy Coler,
    Amy DeAngelis, Pete Fornatale, Matt Hannafin, Kathy Iwasaki, Kevin J. MacDonald,
    Vic Peterson, Terri Sheehan, Marvin Van Tiem.

Contents

Welcome
to the
World
of the

part one

Iguana

External Features of the Iguana

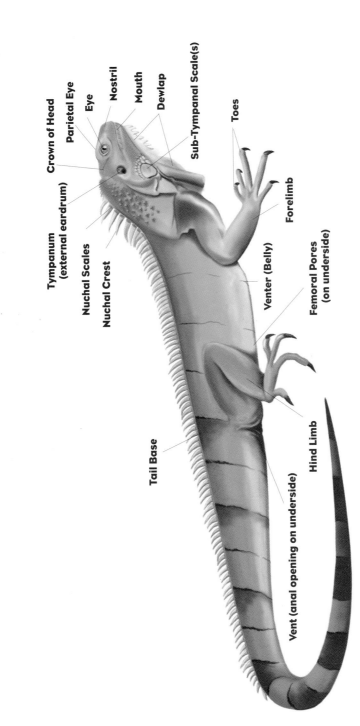

Tympanum
(external eardrum)

Crown of Head

Parietal Eye

Eye

Nostril

Mouth

Dewlap

Sub-Tympanal Scale(s)

Toes

Forelimb

Nuchal Scales

Nuchal Crest

Venter (Belly)

Femoral Pores
(on underside)

Tail Base

Hind Limb

Vent (anal opening on underside)

chapter 1

What Is an Iguana?

The very first thing to realize is that the iguana we are the most familiar with as a pet and the one to which most of this book is dedicated is just one of many species of iguana. Scientifically, it's known as *Iguana iguana*; commonly, it's called the green iguana; familiarly, it's the iguana. Most of the time in this book, when we refer to iguana, we mean the green iguana of pet fame. When we use the term *iguana* to mean the grouping of lizards called iguana, we'll point that out.

Body Type

Iguana lizards range in habitats from arboreal (tree-dwelling) to semiarboreal. Most iguanas have tails that grow from two to three times their actual body length.

5

The iguana is "cold blooded" (technically it is an ecto-therm), meaning its system cannot generate sufficient body heat to sustain itself. It is dependent on outside heat sources to raise its body temperature, which is why it's critical to have the correct environment for an iguana.

Iguanas hatch from eggs (a single clutch may contain as many as sixty eggs). The female lays the eggs deep in a hole that she digs in the ground. The average length of a newborn iguana is about seven inches long. Within a year, it potentially can grow to be about a foot-and-a-half in length. Listed below are some distinguishing body features of the green iguana:

Femoral Pores   On the underside of each back leg, iguanas have a single row of small, circular holes called femoral pores. Usually, the femoral pores of males are significantly larger and more pronounced than those of females. These pores produce a waxy substance that helps the male iguana mark his territory. In most green iguanas, the size of these pores can be used to distinguish males from females.

This head shot of a beautiful mature male green iguana shows the subtympanic scales below the tympanum, the round eye and part of the crest.

Subtympanic Scales   Below the eardrum (tympa-num) of all green iguanas there are one to three greatly enlarged scales.

Parietal Eye   Iguanas have a parietal eye. It is located between the eyes, but a little further toward the back of the head. It does not look so much like a third eye as it does a large gray scale. The parietal eye is sensitive to light cycles, probably aiding in the breeding cycles.

You can see the parietal eye on this mature male iguana. It's the red spot between the two bulges in the middle of the top of the head.

Tongue Iguanas have a short, thick tongue and will attempt to taste or lick a great many things—including their owners! It is normal for the very tip of the tongue to appear to be more red in color than the rest of the tongue.

Teeth An iguana's tooth is round at the root and has ridges on it like a serrated edge. The teeth are described as *pleurodont*, which means that they actually protrude from the jawbone rather than grow from sockets above the jawbone like human teeth.

Crest Both males and females have a row of large pointy scales located down the length of the spine and tail. These scales stand up and retract, and tend to be larger on males than females. When trying to impress females and when fighting with other animals over territory, males will do everything they can to make the crest more pronounced, thus appearing bigger to their opponents.

Dewlap The iguana has a large, hanging fold of skin under its throat called a dewlap. This is expanded and displayed in courtship or in battle. Again, in males they tend to be larger than in females. During mating, females also display their dewlaps.

Color and Size

Individual green iguanas exhibit a variety of shades and colors, depending on what part of Central or South America the iguana originally came from. For example, iguanas from Brazil tend to be more blue, whereas those from El Salvador are a more vivid green, and Mexican iguanas may even be orange. Striped coloring has been noted on iguanas from Guatemala and other Central American countries. Regardless of their original color and pattern, as iguanas age, the colors fade and become more subtle.

Environment

Typically, we think of the green iguana's natural habitat as a tropical environment of lush vegetation and fresh water. But some green iguanas live in more desertlike surroundings and some live near saltwater. Green iguanas are found in areas where temperatures reach 80 to 100 (or even higher) degrees Fahrenheit during the day and drop to 70 degrees Fahrenheit at night.

A day spent with an iguana in Costa Rica, for example, would include feasting on the surrounding vegetation, climbing up trees and vines, basking in a sunny spot, retreating to the shade, feasting on more vegetation, more basking and shading, making its way to a pool or stream for a drink and possibly a swim, a few more nibbles and then a night of sleep. Iguanas are climbers, swimmers, leaf eaters and sunbathers.

Iguanas do have teeth! They use them to chew, of course, and bite. Iguanas use also their tongues a lot to taste and lick things.

How the Iguana Got Its Name

"Iguana" is the interpretation Spanish explorers gave to the name the native American Caribbean Indians called these lizards, which was *iwana*. The word *iguana* was first used by paleontologists to describe a fossil of a prehistoric lizard they found in 1825; they called it an Iguanadon. This was what separated the iguana from other lizards.

This iguana, photographed in Costa Rica, is doing what iguanas love to do: climbing and basking among the lush vegetation in its natural habitat.

All iguanas are included in the family Iguanidae, which contains eight genera, or kinds, of iguanas. These genera include *Amblyrhynchus, Brachylophus, Conolophus, Ctenosaura, Cyclura, Dipsosaurus, Iguana* and *Sauromalus*.

Each of the eight genera includes many species of iguana. Listed below are the more popular varieties of iguana—the ones you can find at your pet store, breeder or zoo. A more complete listing of all the types of iguanids can be found in Chapter 10, "Complete Listing of Iguanas."

Green Iguana *(Iguana iguana)* This is the most commonly kept house pet in the Iguanid family. Although it is most correct to call this animal the green iguana, many people just call it iguana, incorrectly thinking that this is the only lizard called an iguana. And, unless specifically identified in this book, when the word *iguana* is used, it is meant to identify the green iguana.

This species is not in any danger and in fact is enjoying its most prolific period of growth in its history. This iguana is native to Central and South America, ranging all the way from northern Mexico to parts of Paraguay. Iguanas have also been found on islands in the lesser Antilles. Recently, iguanas have been introduced to some parts of the United States, most notably to areas with similar environments (tropical climates with lots of moisture and foliage), such as south Florida.

Of all the iguanas, green iguanas are the most arboreal and were at one time known as "tree iguanas." They are vegetarian reptiles throughout their entire life. Iguanas have been known to eat more than fifty different types of plants, but they prefer to eat the leaves of the types of vegetation found in their environment. As is true of many other reptiles, the iguana is a strong swimmer. Some have been recorded spending a half-hour under water before coming up for air.

This picture shows why green iguanas are called green iguanas! These are healthy, vibrant, youngsters.

A healthy green iguana, given the room to roam and grow, may get to be six to seven feet in length (two thirds of which is tail) and weigh up to twenty-five to thirty pounds. If you allow them to, they will dominate your house. The most important thing to remember with an iguana in regards to its needs is that it is a tropical to semitropical animal, which means it requires warmth, sunlight and humidity for good health. It is diurnal, which means it is active during the daylight hours.

Today, many green iguanas are raised on "farms" in Florida, Texas and some Central American countries.

Depending on what part of Central or South America they are from originally, their color patterns and shades vary. South American iguanas tend to be on the bluer side, while those from Mexico and Guatemala tend to have a more orange hue. Some farms have begun breeding albino stock! These are more yellowish-green than white, but they do have a fair amount of pink in their skin and scales.

Chuckwalla *(Sauromalus obesus)* The chuckwalla is very easy to identify as it looks like a fatter version of the *Iguana iguana*. A native of the southwestern American deserts, the chuckwalla uses its girth to its advantage in the wild. When confronted by an aggressor, the chuckwalla slithers into the narrowest of cracks and then puffs itself up, lodging itself into the rocks so that it cannot be pulled out.

Desert Iguana *(Dipsosaurus dorsalis)* This species is generally smaller than the popular *Iguana iguana*. Found mostly in the southwestern United States and Mexico, it is a desert dweller. There are many state laws that prohibit the capture of wild desert iguanas, and most of the ones that come up for sale to the common hobbyist are bred in captivity by experts.

This is a rhinoceros iguana.

Rhinoceros and Rock Iguanas *(Cyclura spp.)* These iguanas are much larger than the common green iguana. There are many varieties of this particular lizard and it is the largest subset of the iguana family. Although they are extremely handsome lizards, they are also extremely expensive, when available.

Spiny-Tailed or Black Iguana (*Ctenosaura spp.*)

This iguana ranges from Mexico to Panama and is even found on some Colombian islands. The *Ctenosaura* genera lists nine species. They are quite commonly available and some of the rarer species are being bred on farms in several countries. Some are quite affordable.

For the most part, this group tends to be dull-colored, especially as they mature into adults. Even so, there are a few species that are quite visually captivating.

Ctenosaura species are differentiated from other iguanas by their spiny tail. The tail is usually not as long as it is on other iguanas, but is easily distinguished by the winding, sharp, raised scales that protrude from it. Mature adults use this tail as a rather intimidating weapon.

Almost all of the species listed here grow no longer than three feet in length, and, as with most lizards, the females tend to be slightly smaller. Many of these animals are imported, but captive breeding, especially in the United States, is making these species more and more available.

Iguanas in America

For years, iguanas have been popular pets, but few attempts were made to differentiate among the various species. They were always sold under the name *iguana*, regardless if the type was a chuckwalla, a green iguana or a rhinoceros iguana. In the 1950s, iguanas were still being sold under the incorrect name of "Chinese Dragons." In fact, several dinosaur science fiction movies of the 1940s and 1950s actually starred iguanas that were enlarged by trick photography.

> **THREATENED SPECIES**
>
> All iguanas qualify as endangered species, although they vary in degree of endangerment. They are protected under the auspices of CITES (Convention on the International Trade of Endangered Species). This means that they may be sold in their own countries, but if these species are listed as threatened, exporting them between countries requires very extensive permits. This is the reason that many iguanas bought in the United States today are bred here on "farms" or "ranches."

It was not until the 1960s and 1970s that iguanas first drew serious interest and zoologists and experts began to try to separate out the various genera. As the animals gained popularity, iguana breeding farms began to establish themselves, especially in Mexico, Florida and Texas. As late as 1974, there were no reports of iguanas hatching in captivity; probably because no one had tried. But that changed very quickly. Today, green iguanas are the most popular reptile pet in the United States, and most are born and raised on iguana farms.

Where Iguanas Come From Today

Iguana breeding farms have both increased the population of iguanas as well as brought down the price of iguanas. Breeding these reptiles in captivity has also helped people learn more about iguanas, specifically their husbandry needs and their unique and interesting behavior.

There are many advantages to the pet owner of owning farm-bred rather than wild-caught animals. The first and greatest advantage is to the animals themselves. Captured iguanas, born in the wild, usually adapt inadequately to life with people and make poor pets.

Iguanas are by nature timid creatures and tend not to adjust very well to significant changes. When they are forced to live with people, these changes include living in artificial environments and being handled often. They are not used to handlers, and this creates a lot of stress, which may lead the iguana to bite. While some of the bites are not serious, iguanas have teeth and they can draw blood. But the message is clear: Let go and leave me alone! This does not make for a good human-animal relationship. Even more important, these new stresses lead to poor health of the iguana and then, sometimes, its demise. Because of these stresses, a great many wild-caught iguanas stop eating, get sick and die in captivity.

chapter 2

The **World** **According** to the **Iguana**

The iguana is naturally very suspicious toward other animals, human or otherwise, basically because it is concerned with its own safety.

As is true of your relationship with any pet, building trust between you and your iguana is the most important thing to strive for. If you do this correctly and are lucky enough to win over your iguana's confidence, you will have a  friend for years. However, if you are impatient or do not take into account this reptile's unique behavior, you will fail in winning over his trust and will have to work around your iguana's natural fear and trepidation whenever you try to interact with your pet.

Gaining the Iguana's Trust

To begin to establish that trust, ironically, it is important that you provide a place for your iguana to go where it can be alone, no matter what your desires may be. An iguana needs a space of its own. At times, they need to be by themselves and you must respect those feelings if you are to have an enduring relationship. Once an iguana feels comfortable with its surroundings, it will start to trust you, and that's when the real fun begins. This doesn't happen quickly; you will have to be patient and understanding. Sometimes, it will be the iguana who's having trouble and sometimes it will be you. You just need to be patient.

It takes time to establish trust between you and your iguana.

Your world is a very scary place for the iguana. Being a pet owner is like being a parent. There are times when you are disappointed or your expectations are not met. Don't get angry with either the iguana or yourself. Both of you are doing the best you can.

Reading Body Language

The very cautious nature of an iguana is borne out by studying the animal's posture and positioning. By understanding this, you can gain insight into what the iguana is thinking. Is he afraid? Does he run away every time you enter the room, or does he move slowly and with confidence? Does he sit there, unmoving? You must learn to read his body language just like you would if you walked into a room and spied a growling

German Shepherd you didn't know. You'd move pretty carefully until you knew him better and he knew you better. Movement and body language are very important to your pet iguana.

A New Kind of Pet

An iguana is not a puppy or a kitten or a gerbil. And it cannot be treated like a puppy, a kitten or a gerbil. Rough-and-tumble tactics may be fine for the new puppy but are definitely not for the iguana. It does not want to wrestle with you on the floor. Iguanas don't wrestle. When they are aggressive, they aren't playing, and either you or the iguana can get hurt if you don't give your pet some space.

Especially in the beginning of your relationship with your iguana, this is extremely important to remember. If you don't want your iguana to be afraid of you, then don't play football with it. Be gentle, calm, slow and steady in your movements. No quick movements! No running around! No throwing it up in the air! No shouting, screaming or blaring stereos! Gentle, slow and quiet are the key words in any iguana's happy, healthy life.

Allow your iguana the space and time to itself that it thrives on, especially when you first bring it home.

Your iguana requires its own space. It needs time to be alone. Iguanas, by nature, are not very social animals. When your iguana enters your home, you are excited. You just got your first iguana. Have patience; you're going to have it a long time, provided that you take care of it well. Don't handle it too often immediately after you have obtained it. Some physical contact is important, but don't smother it with affection.

Iguanas' behavior can range from reserved to aggressive to comical when they are confident of their

17

surroundings. If you provide safety and a sense of calm, and if you are patient and give your iguana enough time to be alone, you will enjoy a healthy pet. The more safety the iguana feels, the less timid it will be.

Think of what our response would be to another human being who constantly wanted to touch us and be all over us, hovering over our every action. Most of us would go crazy in a few short days. Your iguana would do the same, but in a shorter amount of time. Give your pet enough space to feel alone and safe.

Perfect Isn't Possible

It is very important that you understand that even if you do everything correctly and give your pet its own space and time to be alone, there are going to be periods where your iguana is upset, nervous, excited, or aggressive. Don't panic; you didn't fail. Give your iguana more space and start over again slowly and patiently.

In nature, iguanas are solitary beings, living quiet lives. They are more than happy to be left alone most of the time.

How the Iguana Sees Things

It is crucial to remember that your iguana is not a social being. In the wild, iguanas are solitary reptiles, living a quiet life, rarely interacting with other animals. The iguana would be more than happy to be alone most of its life. In fact, it is best to have only one pet iguana per enclosure. It's not that the iguana wants no contact with human beings; it is just that sometimes we want too much.

Loud noises and sudden actions are an absolute no-no. Iguanas may interpret these noises or movements as threats or violence. And no parties! The iguana does not make for a good college fraternity mascot. Keep your pet in an area that is quiet and undisturbed.

When you go to pick up your iguana, don't expect him to run over and jump into your arms like a dog or cat would. Your movements should be slow and graceful. If your iguana is small, gently place your hand under the body and pick him up. If your iguana is larger, make sure you support both his body and tail. Also do not make any harsh sounds in front of your iguana. Don't make loud noises or bark, meow, squeal or hiss—or anything your pet might construe as hostile or predatory.

Most iguanas eventually become comfortable with your presence and your attempts to handle them. It's important not to overreact around iguanas.

Discover Your Iguana

Because almost all iguanas are initially fearful of their human companions, you must be prepared to go through a slow process in order to win over their confidence and establish trust. By doing this, you set the stage for a wonderful, long-term relationship. With luck and lots of patience, you will have an iguana that is calm and comfortable around people. Even if you do everything right, there is always the chance that you'll have an iguana that is too overwhelmed by human interaction to be relaxed around people.

When the new iguana arrives in your household, you will have to work with it and then simply wait and see if all of your patience is rewarded. If your iguana does not become more accepting of you and human interaction, then you may have to change your expectations of this iguana as a pet. You do not necessarily need to find another home for a difficult iguana, but you may need to change how you handle your pet. There is nothing more debilitating to an iguana than engaging in futile handling and petting. It's frustrating for both you and your pet.

Eventually, it will be obvious if your iguana is responding to your attempts to habituate it to people. If you have a tractable animal, in time, it will become more and more comfortable with your attempts to handle him. If you have a fearful iguana, each time you approach, he will either freeze in place and shut his eyes or attempt to flee. As your iguana matures, he will go through changes in attitude and behavior.

It is important to remember that no matter how excited or afraid your iguana is initially, don't overreact. Even the most excitable iguana can eventually become a charming pet.

What to Do with a Difficult Iguana

If your iguana is not responding to your patient attempts at interaction, don't get depressed. The first thing to do is to carefully examine the environment from your iguana's point of view.

- Is there another pet in the house which is intruding in your iguana's space?

- Is the aquarium or cage too close to something noisy, such as an electric appliance like a refrigerator, which makes strange sounds in the middle of the night?

- Maybe your iguana can see his own image and think it's another iguana.

When your iguana is not favorably responding to your attempts at communication, remember to assess the situation from your iguana's perspective. When you start thinking like an iguana, you'll have come a long way to solving the problem and making him a happy, healthy pet.

It may take months before your iguana is comfortable with the stressful environmental changes it endures when it lives in a cage. Hopefully, the more stress-free living you can provide, the sooner your iguana will be able to interact with people.

Personality Types

Basically, there seem to be two types of iguanas—those that, with proper care and development, become one of the most wonderful pets ever known to man; and the high-strung, nervous iguana that may never calm down. Every iguana has its own personality. Given the same basic training, development, environment and patience, some iguanas will be easy to handle and some may never be. Iguanas, like people, are who they are.

It is important to remember that iguanas, like people and other pets, can change their behavior over the years. Hopefully, this change is always for the better. Signs of progress with your iguana include easier accessibility, a relaxed disposition, and a more comfortable demeanor. But one also should realize that a calm iguana may become less easy to handle or even aggressive over time.

Positive Handling

New iguana owners are always trying to handle their pets. And although it is important to develop the trust so necessary in the human-iguana relationship, there are better ways than constant handling to establish that connection. One of them is by hand feeding.

Hand feeding leads to a positive interaction between you and your new friend. Remember that young iguanas will sometimes innocently confuse your fingers with food, but this is usually just a temporary stage and not to be considered an intentional attack. As the trust in your relationship grows, the iguana begins to see you not as an intruder, but as a benefactor—a positive being in its new life.

What makes your iguana become friendlier? In the beginning of your relationship, it is extremely important that the iguana be given some short period of time, maybe a couple of days to a week, before handling starts. Give your pet a chance to develop its confidence level before you approach it. Give your iguana the opportunity to acclimate to its new environment.

Although leaving your iguana in a glass aquarium or in a cage all day is a way for it to have its own space, ignoring it is not being a good iguana owner. You need to carefully observe the body language of your iguana. Is it frightened? Does it stay in one corner of the cage or aquarium? Are there places inside the habitat that are causing your pet stress? If so, you need to remedy these problems, or your iguana will be nervous and harder to handle. Even if progress is moving slowly, you're doing something right. It's only when there's no progress that you need to rethink your approach.

Hopefully, iguanas come to regard their human companions as benefactors, not intruders.

Iguana People

Let's face it—there are iguana people and then there is everybody else. "Everybody else" are those people who see an iguana or see someone outside with their pet iguana and think to themselves: "Ugh!" Non-iguana people see your pet as that green, ugly, creepy, disgusting, vile, cold-blooded reptile. To them you have this prehistoric dinosaur as a pet, which is probably dangerous. It doesn't play fetch. It's probably vicious and kills other animals. Maybe it even eats small children whenever it gets the chance—almost anything imaginable.

If you want a pet that will make lots of noise and slobber all over you, then you are not an iguana person. Iguana people don't see their pets in exactly the same light. To them, the iguana is the most interesting animal on the face of the earth. At times, it has slow, controlled, graceful movements and a calm demeanor; its dignity and silence are all attributes that only iguana people can see. At other times, its frenzied, tail-swishing activities are exciting. Charming and funny, this unique animal is not for everyone—it is only for the discerning.

Unfortunately, not all iguanas want to be pets and most are not trainable the way a dog is. You may need the patience of a saint just to train your iguana to put up with you. Tricks take even longer. Iguanas, like people, have minds of their own and they don't particularly care what is on yours.

When It Doesn't Work

Sometimes, new iguanas are apprehensive and act out of fear; that is understandable. As your relationship develops, hopefully your pet's fear lessens, and eventually a friendship and trust ensues resulting in a tractable iguana. However, even if you have done everything correctly and are calm and patient, you may still have an aggressive or frightful reptile. At this point, you may want to consider selling or giving the animal to someone who is interested in taking on the charge of a problem iguana. Sometimes, just a change of environment or a change of people makes a huge difference in an iguana's life and outlook. Don't feel bad; your problem pet may be someone else's golden child.

The Other Pets— There's a Difference

As stated previously, iguanas are not like other pets, especially mammals. They are different from dogs and cats and birds in many respects. Most importantly, puppies and kittens do not consider you to be a threat.

Right from the start, your pet iguana is not sure what to make of you. It may actually be thinking, "I don't know what that thing is, but I sure hope it doesn't try to eat me." Your dog or cat never thinks like that. That is why your iguana does not come running to meet you at the door.

The iguana lives its life in fear until otherwise convinced that

To iguana lovers, these animals are the most interesting on the face of the earth.

you mean no harm. That's why it's important to provide the iguana with safe quarters and a place to be alone while you gain its trust. Handling comes much later. When your iguana is scared or afraid, do not try to handle or pet it. This only increases its fear.

Don't expect too much too soon from a new iguana. Initially, the important signs of progress are a lack of fear when you enter the room and a willingness to be handled. A young iguana may be prone to fits of panic, tail-whipping, biting, or running. Hopefully, the young iguana will outgrow these temper tantrums, especially once it becomes more comfortable with its environment. If you think your iguana is progressing too slowly, one thing you might consider is rearranging the environment. You can change the position of the aquarium, the light, the objects inside the enclosure, or even the traffic patterns through the room. Sometimes simple changes like these make a world of difference. Remember, iguana owners need to have lots of patience, especially with young iguanas.

Just like all animals, it is normal for iguanas to go through "stages" as they mature. So if you notice some unusually aggressive behavior, it may just be temporary; please don't think your iguana has changed for the worse forever.

Growth Stages

As your iguana gets older, it will go through different stages of behavioral development. At each stage, different character traits become evident. But the animal's inherent personality cannot be "improved upon" or "trained."

When you obtain an iguana, you may be obtaining an individual that has a nasty character, or a sweet, mellow disposition or a combination of the two. Or it may have a fearful character, or a dull character, or be a loner, or a mean nasty critter, or a comedian or a curious and friendly fellow. And one iguana can be all of the above! And each of these traits can come out during the different stages of development.

There are marked differences between the behavior of the baby iguana, the teenage iguana and the adult iguana. They, like other animals, go through stages where they will act very differently than they did in their previous stage. But make no mistake about it; most iguanas have innate dispositions that cannot be altered through training or handling.

Just like each snowflake is unique, each iguana has its own unique disposition. Happy baby iguanas can suffer the terrible twos just like a toddler, and eventually, just like toddlers, they will grow out of that stage. Also, any change in the house, from the cleaning products you use to where you place the couch, may result in changes in your iguana's personality.

If your iguana suddenly starts acting strange, note the behavior change on your calendar and keep track of it. Think about what could be causing it and what else in the environment changed at that time. If it doesn't improve, talk to an experienced iguana owner or consult a veterinarian.

As does any pet, iguanas suffer accidents and problems that require special care and may necessitate professional medical treatment. Just like other pets, iguanas can get hurt or lost. It is your responsibility to minimize any chance of these horrible things happening to your iguana.

Compatibility with Other Iguanas

Few iguanas can live with other iguanas. There are obvious reasons and not so obvious reasons. There may be open aggression and fights between iguanas.

Sometimes males fight; sometimes females fight; sometimes males and females fight. The possibility of trouble always looms.

Territorial battles are the most violent and sometimes they can be fatal. Even long-time roommates might kill one another on any given day. Importantly, iguanas that seem on the surface to be getting along may not be so happy together. One iguana can dominate another iguana to the extent that the subordinate iguana does not eat well, does not feel well and is suppressed and becomes ill. Most iguanas are best kept as solitary pets, away from other iguanas and other reptiles.

Some iguanas get along fine with other iguanas; most do not.

Iguanas are very territorial. Aggressive females have been known to harass male iguanas. In fact, territorial challenges to their human companions are not unknown. Territorial fights can be one of the biggest problems with owning these wonderful lizards. In many cases, separation to different parts of the house is the only way to alleviate the tension. This may require that one iguana is removed from the sight of another for a lifetime.

Some people have been known to keep other lizards in the same environment with iguanas, but this is not recommended. Just think: If iguanas view you as a competitor or as a predator, what must they think of other lizards or iguanas? It is important to note that wild iguanas are solitary creatures and only socialize during the breeding season. During that time, the males fight violently for the right to breed. That's why it is always best to keep one iguana per enclosure. Iguanas are truly happier alone.

Make sure your iguana gets regular exposure to real sunlight.

Dispelling Myths

Probably because keeping iguanas as pets is relatively new, there are a lot of myths about how to raise and care for them. This book will dispel a lot of them, and as you get into the feeding and habitat chapters you'll learn how to do things right for your iguana. Because you will inevitably hear a lot of different advice, we're providing this checklist for your reference. We hope it keeps you from worrying unnecessarily, and keeps your iguana safe from harm.

- Iguanas with orange skin are not necessarily sick. Sometimes their skin will appear orange, but it may be no cause for concern. However, if the skin turns orange/yellow over a very short amount of time and the iguana is also showing signs of sickness (lethargy, not eating), consult a veterinarian immediately.

- Iguanas are not deaf, as some experts have suggested, and it is thought that they can identify color.

- Iguanas are exceptionally smart pets. Let one loose in your house and see if you can find it. Who's smarter?

- A small area to live in will not produce a smaller animal, only an uncomfortable animal. If you keep an iguana in a small cage it will only get more cramped as it gets older.

- Make sure your pet gets real sunlight (not filtered through a window) whenever possible, and use the correct spectrum of ultraviolet lighting to give your pet the best possible substitute when you can't give it sunlight. Artificial lighting is not a replacement; it is a substitute.

- Feeding your iguana dog food will not make it more aggressive. But because, in the wild, they eat no animal protein, *iguanas should not be fed any food that has animal protein as part of its ingredients.* No one knows for sure, but some experts think that kidney disease in iguanas may be due to feeding them animal protein as they are growing in their early years. Kidney disease is becoming a more and more common problem in iguanas, which is truly sad. Iguanas cannot be trusted to eat what is good for them. They will eat anything they can find or that is given to them.

- Some experts will tell you that handling or petting the iguana for fifteen minutes a day guarantees he will be tame. Other experts will say that you have to handle the iguana every day for him to get to know or like you. Don't believe them. Every iguana is an individual and they don't always read the rule book!

Temperament and Sex

Male and female iguanas have very different temperaments. It is generalized that males can be more aggressive and independent, and less overtly curious. Generally, the female seems less likely to be interested in investigating the house and would rather be trying to find a hiding spot.

*Some people
prefer females
because they tend
to be calmer and
easier to work
with than males.*

ABOUT FEMALES

Some iguana owners prefer female iguanas. Usually females are more sedate, and this is the type of behavior that most people like best about the iguana. Some individuals prefer the challenge of a male iguana. But whichever you prefer, appreciate each animal for its own unique personality.

Some people dislike female iguanas because they feel they tend to be more timid and remain more aloof than males. Females are more sensitive to noise and quick movement. But it is not uncommon to find those females that become dominant attempt or succeed in dominating males. Generally, once tamed, females tend to be easier to handle than males.

For those people with less patience, the female tends to be the better pet, as she may be easier to tame and more sedate than males.

ABOUT MALES

An aggressive male iguana is an amazing sight to see. Within a matter of seconds, it can go from sitting quietly on the table to a tail-swishing, jumping, lunging, mouth-gaping scaled ball of fury.

Males are definitely more aggressive than females. They have many assertive traits that can be either positive or negative, depending on your point of view. But a calm male is as easy to handle and travel with as any calm female.

Males, on the whole, tend to be more active than females. Once your male iguana feels secure in your home he will want to go everywhere, and nothing will stop him from investigating. However, this requires more attention and more supervision on your part. Also, males tend to want to patrol their territory and defend it staunchly. Some males are less likely to perform these "duties," but the true dominant male will be ever on the lookout for other opposing males, ready to do battle.

Male iguanas tend to be more self-assured and want to patrol their territory.

As compared to females, even the less aggressive of the males are very active and inquisitive. During the majority of the day, even the most aggressive of males are happy to be fed and lie underneath a heat lamp or in the sun. But you will find some males that are perpetually mellow, preferring not to travel, and who don't mind occasional contact with humans. Just don't interrupt their schedule. However, if travel is necessary, they will make a good show of it. These are the kind of iguanas that would prefer to age gracefully, leaving the dominating to others.

MALE HEAT

Once a year, some dominant males will get into what some people call "male heat." This is a temporary condition, which generally lasts two months depending on the area of the country you are in. This behavior is due to the dominant male's aggressive personality and sexual assertiveness.

Many owners interpret this activity to mean that their animal is turning against them, but this is not the case. Aggressive Iguanas strike quickly; the male in heat will simply move more deliberately to satisfy himself.

What happens to a male iguana in "heat"? This only happens to some males—those that are particularly dominant and territorial. They become especially restless, often pacing around their cage or a room. This is because the territorial instinct becomes even stronger when the mating instinct hits.

These males will try to find a substitute if they cannot mate a female. The substitute could be your finger, arm or leg, and it doesn't matter whether you are a man or a woman. Just as when a dog "humps" his owner's leg, the iguana will try to grab on to your appendage and begin to mate with it. This is very alarming, especially if you're caught unaware.

Between iguanas, if the female tries to escape from the male, he increases his efforts to hold on to her. The same thing will happen if you try to quickly separate yourself from your iguana. The best thing to do is push your fingers against the iguanas eyes—not so hard that you cause serious harm, but enough to cause some distracting pain.

Male "heat" lasts two to three months. During this time, it's best to avoid handling your male, and keep him separated from other iguanas.

chapter 3

Choosing
Your
Iguana

A pet shop is the most common place for beginners to go to obtain an iguana. The problem is that it is impossible to gauge the reptile expertise of most pet shop salespeople. The information they provide will vary from store to store. In a perfect world, local pet shops have an interest in maintaining a good relationship with their customers, and salespeople should try to correctly answer all your questions; when they can't answer a question, they should refer you to an expert. Unfortunately, their answers may be wrong due to ignorance or a lack of up-to-date information.

The purpose of this chapter is to give you an idea of what to look for before you walk into the pet store so you can ask knowledgeable questions. The store personnel should work with you to help you find the right iguana, and if you don't feel comfortable with their advice, you should probably go to another store.

What to Look For

PHYSICAL TRAITS

If you suspect an iguana you're interested in was captured in the wild, pass on it. These iguanas take a long time to tame.

A healthy iguana is active and has a full, thick tail base. When iguanas are sick and lose weight, the tail base becomes thin and the bones almost protrude through the skin. The best age to purchase a pet iguana is when they are three to five months old because they are strong enough to withstand change but young enough to adjust to changes in their environment. Iguanas younger than three months may not be sufficiently strong enough to adapt to the physical or psychological hardships of change.

Baby iguanas range in size from about one and a half to seven inches in length (head to rear legs). You want a new healthy iguana to be thin, bright green and alert.

Babies are inquisitive and are not afraid of being handled, though it's important not to overhandle them when you bring one home. In a healthy baby iguana, the body must be taut and sinewy. They are active, not lethargic.

If the baby looks bloated, whether in the limbs or in the stomach, then avoid it; this is usually a sign that there is something seriously wrong. If there are any swellings along the jaw, avoid that iguana. There should be no discharge around the nose or mouth and there should be no evidence of burns on the skin.

OLDER VERSUS YOUNGER ANIMALS

In general, babies are usually more active and more tame than adults. When you're inspecting baby iguanas from the pet shop, make sure there are no quick movements or loud voices, and avoid rough handling.

You may see adults in the pet shop. Literally and figuratively, approach these older iguanas with caution. Some of these older iguanas may be previously owned pets that are now in the pet store because of unacceptable behavior traits. Ask the salesperson about the animal's health and behavior and ask why an adult is for sale.

Older iguanas may have been captured in the wild and brought to the store. With an increasing number of breeding farms around the country, fortunately, the presence of these wild iguanas in pet stores is becoming rarer. These are usually not good pets for beginners. Raised in the wild, they take a long time to tame and habituate to the domestic setting and are best left to experts.

Healthy baby iguanas are bright green, skinny and alert, with smooth skin.

CHARACTER TRAITS

Whether a baby or an adult, the first thing you should analyze is the fear quotient. Is the baby or the adult frozen with fear when a person approaches? If so, don't buy it. You should be allowed to hold the iguana at the pet shop. If it doesn't move, doesn't lick you and has its eyes closed, then this is not your iguana.

You want an iguana that keeps moving in a steady, not neurotic, fashion. If an iguana stretches in front of you the first time that it sees you, that's a comfortable, well-adjusted, confident iguana. Take that iguana!

You should also slowly, gently stroke the iguana along the length of its back to see how it reacts to human contact. Any sudden movements by the iguana may be an indication of its willingness to run and its discomfort with people. If the clerk will let you, you may also want to see if the iguana will stay on your forearm. If it does, then this is also a good sign that it is used to people.

You want an iguana that willingly approaches its food bowl, not one that seems fearful of everything.

THE SKIN

One of the most important things to look for when choosing a healthy iguana is the skin color and texture. Baby iguanas should normally have bright green skin, no matter what part of the world they are from. Very rarely they can be blue-green, which is normal for that color variation. However, most importantly, you are looking for color vibrancy.

The colors, no matter what shade, should be intense. Any dull, pasty or pale-looking iguanas should be quickly discarded from consideration. Also, any iguana that has a yellowish-green hue should not be purchased, as this coloration may indicate impending illness.

As iguanas grow in size and age they lose their intense color and become a grayish green. Some will change to a reddish-orange color, which is very much in demand. But whether you're looking at a baby or an older iguana, you'll be able to tell if the skin is healthy by the overall tone of the colors and the elasticity and texture of the skin.

The skin should not hang from the iguana's sides or belly. There should be no scars or open wounds on the iguana. If there are dark areas on the skin, these may be indications of previous injuries, such as those sustained from burns or fights.

If the iguana is shedding, that is not a problem. That indicates he is growing, which means he is eating, implying that he is at least a little more comfortable with his surroundings than other iguanas his age. If he is shedding, make certain the skin underneath looks healthy.

> **THE FINGER TEST**
>
> This is a simple character test you can conduct on a store iguana. While you're handling an iguana, hold your finger to its mouth. A lick is a sign of submission; a good thing for a pet iguana. A bite might indicate a more aggressive animal, but that's no reason to reject it; this animal may just be hungry. If the iguana is frozen in place, it is probably very afraid.

EYES

An iguana's eyes should not be wide open; their eyes should be relaxed and clear. Wide-open eyes indicate fear or apprehension. The eyes should also not be closed. This may mean eye disease or even that the iguana is ill and too sick to open its eyes. Look for any scars on the surface of the eye.

LICKING

If the iguana you have your eye on sticks its tongue out and starts licking you, it shows that you have a confident, secure animal in front of you. If it doesn't lick you voluntarily, put your finger near its mouth and see if it will lick you. If it does, that's also a good sign. Does it lick when it walks? That's a good sign, too. An iguana will not lick when it is scared or intimidated.

Sometimes a baby will lick your finger and then bite it. That's understandable in babies. It's just confusing

your finger with food. It's also a good sign because it
says that your choice has a healthy appetite.

Carrying the Iguana Home

Once you've chosen your iguana, you'll need to think
about how to get it home. The shop specialist will probably recommend a carrier of some sort. If it's a plastic
bag, pass. Some experts argue that placing your pet in
a plastic bag can be frightening as the plastic smells
and it is clear. You want to keep your iguana feeling
safe and secure for the rest of its life, so start right away.
A covered cardboard box with holes in it makes a safe,
secure carrier. Bring it with you to the store to carry
the animal home in. You want your iguana to be quiet,
and a dark box is just what you need.

*A healthy
iguana's eyes
will be relaxed
and clear.
Wide-open eyes
indicate fear.*

A Checklist of What to Look
for in a New Iguana

AGE AND SIZE

You want a young iguana, three to five months old, five
to seven inches long. These are usually less afraid,
more curious, and have an easier time adjusting to
domesticated life. It will be easier in the long run
to tame these younger animals. Beginners should stick
to younger iguanas, and not try to take on troublesome
animals probably in need of expert care.

SKIN

You want a bright green color, not unlike the new shoots of a plant. You should not buy an iguana who looks waxy, pale or yellowish, as this is a sign of sure death.

BODY

You want an iguana who shows no signs of physical damage, and who has a thick tail-base and lean, sinewy body. You should not buy an iguana with wounds of any kind.

BEHAVIOR

You want an alert iguana who doesn't run when you approach the aquarium. It should show some interest in you, and should have smooth movements. It should not be frozen with its eyes shut or running around trying to find an escape hatch.

APPETITE

You want an iguana who's hungry when the food dish is set down, or who will take food from your hand. Don't buy an iguana who's not interested in food.

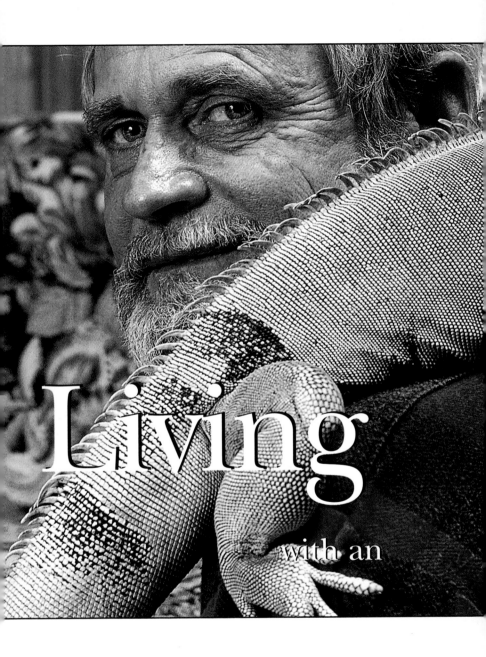

Living

with an

part two

Iguana

chapter 4

Bringing
Your **Iguana**
Home

How you house your iguana is the key to how well you maintain the health of your iguana.

It is important to remember that, in the wild, iguanas have the ability to range over a large territory. They are relatively active and walk and swim and climb. Males especially are constantly canvassing their territories looking out for competitive males. Obviously you can't offer up the house to your iguana, but there are ways to compromise to keep both your iguana and you happy.

Housing Requirements

This is a list of the most basic requirements for housing your iguana. Details on setting up and outfitting your iguana's habitat are explained later in the chapter.

SPACE

One of the basic requirements that you need to consider is space. An iguana needs space to roam and a space to hide. A safe enclosure must be provided so that the iguana cannot escape and so nothing can get into your iguana's cage. It is heartbreaking when an iguana crawls out of its enclosure and gets either lost or hurt.

Also, it is of the utmost importance that nothing be allowed to threaten your iguana, especially other house pets. The common house cat, for example, is largely responsible for the dwindling iguana populations in the Caribbean. The iguana's living space should also be a safe distance from loud noises or away from the household traffic.

Iguanas will want to stay under a heat lamp for long periods of time.

TEMPERATURE

Another important, basic consideration is temperature. Because the iguana is an ectotherm (cold-blooded animal), it depends on the ambient temperature to regulate its internal temperature. An iguana must have an area inside its enclosure that reaches temperatures of 85 to 100 degrees Fahrenheit, especially during the day. The temperature should not fall below 70 degrees Fahrenheit.

Younger iguanas, especially the babies, may want to stay under the heat lamps both day and night. Adults may not exhibit this need, as they are quite comfortable lowering their body temperatures at night.

But you don't want to bake your iguana, either. Be sure there's a place in the enclosure where the iguana can go to get out of the heat, whether it's a corner away from a heat source or a ledge to hide under. Place a thermometer in the basking area to be certain that the heated area is not getting too hot for your iguana.

ENVIRONMENT

Just like you, the iguana is comfortable when it is comfortable with its surroundings. Iguanas are more happy when their enclosures include things like tree limbs, places to hide, an elevated shelf or two, and maybe even a large dish or giant bowl of water. A cardboard or wooden box placed in the enclosure will satisfy an iguana's need to hide when it is scared and provide a place to sleep comfortably at night.

HOW CLOSE TO THE LIGHT?

Whether you are using incandescent, reflector or full-spectrum bulbs, the standard safe distances should apply:

A 75-watt bulb should be one and a half feet away from basking area;

A 100-watt bulb should be two feet away;

A 150-watt bulb should be at least two and a half to three feet away, depending on household temperatures.

The very best place to situate your iguana's enclosure is by a window where it might get exposure to sunlight. But remember, the ultraviolet light spectrum so needed by iguanas for their health does not go through the glass in the windows. *Being by a window is not a substitute for direct exposure to sunlight or artificial ultraviolet light.*

An elevated perching area will make an iguana feel better. It gives him the sense of natural safety that all tree-climbing animals crave.

LIGHT

Lighting is another basic consideration that must be addressed before bringing a new iguana into your home. An iguana cannot thrive if it is kept in a dark room all day. If you live in a warm area of the country, your pet needs to be in direct sunlight (not through a window of any kind) as much as possible. If it cannot be in direct sunlight, it must have as much artificial ultraviolet lighting as possible.

Iguanas need to be near sources of natural light for at least some part of the day. This one is getting direct sun through a window screen.

FOOD AND WATER

Just like all living things, iguanas require water and the correct diet to live a long life. An important rule to remember is not to feed it what it wants; feed it what it needs. A very basic diet recommendation includes a variety of vegetables and plant materials and a very small amount of fruits. It is important to avoid iceberg lettuce as there is little nutritional value in this food. (More on this subject in Chapter 5, "Feeding Your Iguana.")

A bowl of water is mandatory. Depending on the size of the bowl, your iguana may want to bathe in it. That's fine; just remember to wash it and fill it back up with cool, clean water. In fact, you may want to provide a water bowl for drinking and a larger water bowl for swimming.

What Kind of Enclosure?

Most people prefer to initially house their baby iguana in an aquarium. As the iguana grows, people will change to larger enclosures. Although birdcages are usually bigger and offer more space to roam, baby iguanas are small enough to slip through the bars. Observe your baby closely and see what it can or cannot do. That will determine the size of the initial enclosure you will need for your new pet.

Regardless of which kind of enclosure you choose, never allow your baby iguana to roam around the house unsupervised. There are too many places in your house in which it could be injured or lost. Crawl spaces and heating vents are your biggest enemies.

Baby iguanas can be kept in aquariums while they are still small, but not forever!

AQUARIUMS VERSUS CAGES

There are good and bad aspects about aquariums. They can be heavy and difficult to move. Another problem is due to the glass, which blocks the beneficial rays of the sun and also intensifies the heat. Sometimes this can cause a burn on your iguana's skin or, if it gets hot enough, your iguana can die from heat exposure.

Aquariums, being enclosed on five of six sides, can potentially lead to unsanitary conditions. They may be difficult to clean, especially if moisture accumulates in the substrate. Also, if there are unsanitary conditions, the odor level will greatly increase, making for some unpleasant living conditions for both your iguana and your nose. Actually, this is a serious condition, as odors that increase in this closed environment may be toxic to your iguana's respiratory system, predisposing him to respiratory diseases.

Foliage supplies a lot of the iguana's needs—shelter, food, hiding places and the sense of being in a natural environment.

Most baby iguanas are small enough to be housed in a thirty-gallon tank, but when the iguana starts to grow, both you and the iguana will prefer another type of enclosure. When an iguana grows beyond thirty inches (including the length of the tail) you really need to build a large cage or pen. At that point, you're talking about an animal larger than a cat or a toy dog, and you wouldn't keep either of them in an aquarium.

A cage offers the best possible air circulation and does not interfere with the light from the sun. If the cage is tall enough, you can add shelves or branches for the iguana to climb on. Cages are also less likely to break and are lighter to carry.

It is important that iguanas have enough space to feel comfortable. A six-foot animal obviously needs something much larger than a six-inch one. For adult iguanas in warmer areas of the country, many enthusiasts have outdoor enclosures for the day and smaller inside ones for sleeping at night.

A four-foot-long iguana would require a cage with dimensions of six feet (height) by six feet (width) by thirty inches (depth). Cages or pens can be easily built and casters are put on the cages so that they are easily moved.

An advantage to cages is that because they are easier to move than glass enclosures, you can take them out on a nice day and put them in the yard so that your iguana can get some natural sunlight. That bountiful natural sunlight will be a big treat. A special note to remember, though: Do not leave the cage unattended as you never know what neighborhood pets or wild animals are around to harass your little green friend. Always make sure you are there for the iguana.

These two iguanas live in a specially outfitted cage. But it is best not to have more than one iguana per enclosure.

Equipping the Cage

Iguanas look for height and they need sun. Iguanas also like to cool off in shady areas—they need plants, and they need water. Their craving for climbing can be solved by placing a tree limb, branch or even a shelf somewhere in the enclosure. Iguanas naturally want to climb, and once they've ascended, they like to rest there and soak up sunlight. The limb you put in the iguana's cage should always be one-and-a-half to two times larger than your iguana.

Foliage is important because it provides shade when the animal wants to cool down. It also provides a hiding space to camouflage the iguana if intimidated by sudden movements or a guest. Unfortunately, iguanas will eat all plants you put in with them, so you may need to be continually replacing this cage "ornament."

ORGANIC OR FAKE FLOWERS

To protect your iguana from poisons, the plants should not have been exposed to pesticides. One of the best plants to place with your iguana is the Wandering Jew. Be certain that it has not been exposed to pesticides and be certain that you are not very attached to the plant, as your iguana will eat it in due time.

Do not put common household plants in with your iguana unless you have checked with your veterinarian. Some of the common household plants are toxic to iguanas and other animals. So, to be on the safe side, no houseplants in the enclosure.

There is no shame in using plastic plants in your iguana's cage. They will inevitably be sampled, but not eaten. They can be washed and re-used if they get soiled, and they provide your pet with shade and camouflage comfort.

Should You Let Your Iguana Out?

WHY YOU SHOULDN'T

As your iguana gets older, tamer and more accustomed to you, you may be tempted to allow it to roam around the house. There are many reasons not to give in to this temptation. When iguanas roam the house, they can get hurt, as few people iguana-proof their house. To this extent, you need to directly supervise your pet while it is free in the house.

Other than the threat to your iguana's safety, there is another good reason to keep the iguana in its cage. Few homes are warm enough for your iguana's metabolism. Most homes are kept with temperatures in the 70s, and this is too low for an iguana's metabolism and good health. And, if your iguana is meandering around the house, it will not be under the ultraviolet light source you have so nicely set up in his cage. Therefore, your pet will miss out on a vital aspect of his environment.

If you could provide an area where the iguana was able to maintain the high body temperature and be exposed to direct sunlight or ultraviolet light, it would be less dangerous for him to be out of his cage.

If You Do

Many iguanas only want to sit on top of their cages to get closer to the light. Others want to investigate. If you think your iguana is ready to join you and your family in the rest of the house, first find an area that can be closed off and that's completely safe to roam around in, like a spare bedroom or the kitchen. Make sure all sharp objects are cleared away. Make sure anything the iguana can swallow is cleared away.

Iguanas like to climb, and when they're loose in your house will seek high comfortable spots, like the back of the sofa.

Anytime you let an iguana wander, you must keep in mind that they can and will climb almost anything, including drapery, any kinds of cords hanging down, furniture, book cases and so forth. This is not something you want to do with especially young iguanas. A four-foot iguana is hard to lose in your living room; a six-inch lizard is easy to lose in a house.

While some dominant males may want or demand more space by clawing at the door (iguanas aren't dumb), the older iguana is happy just to have the space and the perception of space, as opposed to being cooped up in a cage. They may not move more than a foot in any direction, but that available space is important. And certainly, once your iguana is older, tamer and better adjusted to living with you, you won't mind letting it sit on your shoulder, or walk around a room.

Substrate

NEWSPAPER

Whether you are using a cage or an aquarium, the bottom of the enclosure needs to be lined with something. The most popular and safest lining material is newspaper. Some people place ripped-up or shredded news-

paper on the bottom while others prefer to line the enclosure as they would a birdcage, with flat sheets. Either way, newspaper is the easiest, safest and cheapest way to line the bottom. Another advantage to using newspaper is that it is easy to know when it is soiled and ready to be changed so that your iguana does not walk around in a messy cage.

Astroturf is a substrate some experts prefer because it can be taken out and cleaned off and it looks nice.

PELLETS

Two other preferred substrates are rabbit pellets and alfalfa pellets. Even if your iguana decides to eat this, that's okay; it's edible and even provides nutrients that he needs. They are very absorbent, which keeps the cage looking clean but may fool you into not realizing how dirty the substrate really is.

ASTROTURF

Some people recommend carpeting or Astroturf. Carpeting is not a good idea. It is easily soiled and hard to clean, and the iguana may even try to eat it. Astroturf, on the other hand, works well in most cages.

Many experts use Astroturf and put a small sandbox in the corner. Do not use cat litter, as your iguana will eat it and block its intestines! A little sand in a small dish or bowl is fine. It is also important to note that iguanas sometimes defecate in their water bowl. It is important to change the water every day for this reason.

With Astroturf, you do need to take it out regularly and clean it thoroughly. If you have two pieces of Astroturf that fit the cage, you can take one out and clean it while you replace it with the other spare one. Many experts use this method. As your iguana gets older and you understand his habits better, you may eventually want to change over to this type of substrate.

OTHER TYPES

You may see recommendations for such things as cedar chips, orchid bark or pine shavings. This may give the cage a more natural look than newspaper, but there can be problems if these types of materials are used. Fecal material and food can be buried in the shavings, allowing bacteria and fungi to grow unchecked. Since iguanas are highly susceptible to all kinds of infections and diseases, this buildup of microorganisms is not good for the health of your iguana. Also, the aroma of these shavings, especially cedar chips, may even be toxic to iguanas and other lizards.

Another reason to avoid woodchip substrates is that iguanas will eat these shavings. If your iguana ate this material, it could get an intestinal infection, or worse, a blocked intestine that would necessitate surgery. For these simple reasons many experts avoid wood shavings altogether.

Although realistic, it is not recommended to use dirt or sand as a substrate. Your iguana can ingest this material, causing an infection or, worse, a blockage in the intestines. This is very serious and can lead to the death of your iguana. Also, sand and dirt are not very hygienic. Bacteria and fungal organisms are harbored in this material and can cause disease and death in your iguana.

Regulating the Heat

Iguanas come from areas where temperatures reach the high 80s and 90s and even higher. Being ectotherms, these are temperatures that lizards love. If you are lucky enough to live in an area where your iguana is naturally exposed to these kinds of temperatures, all you need to do is make sure your iguana is getting enough light. However, iguana owners in the rest of the world must recreate temperature conditions to ensure the health of your pet. Over the years, people have tried various methods to bring heat and light into their iguana's manmade environment.

There are basically two ways you can give your iguana heat: (1) with lights (incandescent, reflector and full-spectrum bulbs) and (2) with "hot rocks" and other heating pads. Let's discuss these a little more in detail.

LIGHTS

Reflector and Incandescent Bulbs

The iguana uses warmth to regulate its body temperature, to help in the digestion of food (heat speeds up the digestive process) and basically to perform all of its bodily functions. Most iguana enthusiasts equip an enclosure with one or two lamps placed in strategic locations to provide both heat and light.

The lamps are usually placed outside of the cage, sufficiently far enough away so that the iguana can't be burned no matter how long it basks. The uppermost part of the tree limb or branch in the enclosure should be about eighteen inches away from the bulb.

Most enthusiasts use a 100-watt reflector bulb, or a common 100-watt incandescent bulb, with traditional large aluminum reflectors and attached clamps so that the lights can be securely fastened. The reflectors are more popular because the heat emanating from them can be much more easily directed than the incandescent lights, which tend to emit less heat.

Lights are placed outside the enclosure so the iguana can't get too close and burn itself.

Light bathing a tree limb will enable your iguana to bask when it wants to and then leave to cool off at its own pace. The temperature at this spot should be approximately 93 to 100 degrees Fahrenheit (34 to 38 degrees Celsius). As was discussed earlier, iguanas also need a time to cool off, so it is important that only a part of the enclosure be well heated to keep iguanas healthy. Too much heat is just as bad as not enough.

Lightbulbs should not be placed anywhere near the iguana because iguanas will attempt to sit on or near a lighted bulb. If they are too close to a lighted bulb, they will burn themselves, sometimes very seriously. It is imperative that the iguana not be able to touch or sit too close to a lighted bulb.

Ultraviolet Lights

Iguanas do not only bask in the sun for heat; they need to be exposed to beneficial ultraviolet (UV) rays. By absorbing UV rays from natural sunlight, iguanas are able to synthesize vitamin D_3 to enhance their absorption of calcium. Incandescent or reflector bulbs do not provide these necessary rays. If your iguana cannot be exposed to direct sunlight most of the year, then an artificial source of ultraviolet radiation must be present.

DOES IT WORK?

Several manufacturers have begun selling full-spectrum lighting products, and though they claim the light simulates direct sunlight, the jury of iguana experts is still out on full-spectrum lighting. There is no conclusive proof that full-spectrum lighting emits enough or the correct spectrum of UV rays and, therefore, has any effect on the synthesis of vitamin D_3. You need to give your iguana as much real, direct sunlight as possible.

Since the jury is still out on these full-spectrum bulbs, you should still have an ultraviolet light source in the cage. Current research recommends that iguanas be no more than eighteen inches from the ultraviolet light source. It is best to have this light outside the cage to keep your iguana safe from harm. Also, you may want to consider having numerous UV light sources placed in each area of the enclosure that your iguana basks in.

> **THERMAL BURNS**
>
> Thermal burns are a very common problem for veterinarians to treat. They are caused by iguanas getting too close to heat sources such as lightbulbs or hot rocks. To prevent this, bulbs must be placed outside of the enclosure so that the iguana cannot lie against them. Don't use hot rocks; use other methods to increase the temperature of the enclosure.

HOW MUCH LIGHT?

Because iguanas are diurnal, the light should be left on all day but turned off at night. Baby iguanas are especially fond of the lights and their basking times, and will spend as much time under the lights as possible.

For the first few days you should leave the light on as long as possible and see how your pet reacts. You can then best judge what hours of the day are important for your animal to bask.

HOT ROCKS AND HEATING PADS

One of the most talked-about topics in the iguana world is the hot rock (which is also known as the "sizzle stone"). These are very popular with pet owners, especially in areas where the temperatures are relatively low. The pet shops have plenty of them.

Iguanas love to bask, so it's imperative to set up a good basking spot for your pet.

The hot rock looks like a real rock, but it has a heating element planted inside to provide a warm surface for an iguana to bask on. The iguana can get warm without the lights on. Theoretically, it is a simple idea, as the iguana gets on top of the hot rock to warm itself up and gets off when it's had enough.

Though some hot rocks may work well, there are a great many that either get too hot or get hot only in certain spots. If the iguana gets too hot, your pet will get injured via a thermal burn. Thermal burns are extremely serious injuries and can be life threatening. The best advice is not to use a hot rock.

Other experts simply use different methods to heat the enclosure.

There are heating pads specifically designed for enclosures that are put under the tank to heat it. It may be dangerous to use a common heating pad, and that is not recommended. You can even use something like heat tape placed around the outside of the tank.

Unless you live in the desert, you will need some sort of supplemental heating for your iguana. At this point, it is difficult to recommend hot rocks; if the technology improves in the future, maybe it will be a heating option.

Although some iguanas do sunbathe on rocks, albeit not that often (they prefer the safety of trees), once supplied, iguanas will spend an inordinate amount of time near a hot rock. A hot rock or heating pad, if necessary, should only be located in one area of the enclosure, so there is a place for your lizard to go to cool off.

The hot rock should never be thought of as a main heat source. It is best to remember that there should be a thermal gradient in your enclosure. There should be a basking area where the temperatures approach 100 degrees Fahrenheit and an area where they may get as low as 70 degrees Fahrenheit. Within this gradient, there should be strategically placed UV lights so that your iguana can get the full benefit of those rays. Also, make sure your iguana is not more than eighteen inches from those UV lights to maximize the benefit of them.

Taking your iguana into the sun for an hour or so a day is sufficient, though your iguana wouldn't mind more sun!

Sunlight

In nature, the iguana spends the greatest part of the day basking in the sunlight. That is not because it is a lazy lizard. It needs the warmth and UV radiation to

57

survive. You cannot use sunlight that comes through the window because the glass filters out the crucial UV rays. You can best understand the value of direct, real sunlight on iguanas once you compare those who have had it with those who haven't. The number-one cause of metabolic bone disease in iguanas is lack of UV light due to nonexposure to sunlight. The iguana's system needs the sunlight to synthesize vitamin D_3 to help build its bones. It is the pet owner's responsibility to make sure the iguana is getting as much real, direct sunlight as possible or, in its place, artificial UV light.

The lack of vitamin D_3 due to nonexposure to UV rays leads to a calcium deficiency. Calcium deficiency is first seen in young iguanas as deformities of the legs, the back, the head and the jaw. The bones begin to bend and become misshapen. In the worst cases the bones, especially the backbone, will either bend or break. The saddest part of this disease is that it is preventable.

LET THE SUN SHINE IN

There is no substitute for sunlight, and when at all possible, your iguana should be exposed to real and direct sunlight. No matter how much incandescent light you provide, your iguana will always need real sunlight or ultraviolet lightbulbs. Lack of ultraviolet light is the leading cause of metabolic bone disease. This is one of the iguana owner's highest priorities.

How Much Sun?

Exposing your iguana to real sunlight is not as difficult as it sounds, especially if you live in a warm area of the world. If you take it into the sun for about an hour or so a day, you should be able to maintain a happy, healthy iguana. It is important that baby iguanas get as much real sunlight as possible, as they are highly susceptible to metabolic bone diseases.

There may not be as much benefit taking your iguana out in the winter or colder months. Not only may the iguana not get as much ultraviolet radiation due to the position of the earth, but it will likely be too cold to be safe for your iguana.

Of course, the best thing to do is place your iguana's enclosure near an open window where direct sunlight can reach the animal. It is important in these instances to make sure that the lid to the cage is securely fastened to prevent escape.

THE SUNNING CAGE

Some experts use a sunning cage to get their iguanas sufficient sunlight. A sunning cage can be a small cage that is big enough to house the animal temporarily, is easy to carry, and can be left out on your patio without fear of your pet escaping. The best thing to do is to set the cage on a patio table or bench, giving the iguana the illusion that it is perched up high and is safe. If it is on the ground, your iguana may become very frightened. And make sure the cage is large enough and situated in such a way that it has a covered or shaded area so your iguana can escape the heat.

It is important to remember that the sunning cage must be made safe from other pets or wild animals. The cat next door would love to get to your iguana inside.

chapter 5

Feeding

Your

Iguana

Variety is the spice of life. It is as true for iguanas as it is for people. Imagine eating the same food every night for dinner, whether it be spaghetti or hot dogs or spareribs or pot roast or tuna fish. The same thing night after night. Ugh! Don't expect your iguana to be any happier if he gets the same food night after night. The dietary guidelines at the end of the chapter give detailed information on the various foods iguanas can eat, and what percentages they should comprise in the overall diet.

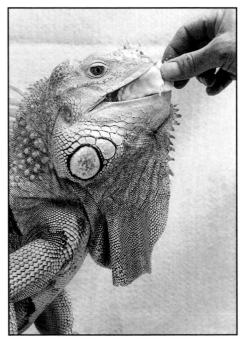

Iguanas are like children. They will eat what they want to eat and not necessarily what is good for them. So it is up to you to monitor their diets closely. They need a balanced diet just like we do. Some iguanas, as they get older, are extremely stubborn and resistant to change. There is the great risk that your iguana would die before changing its eating habits. So it's important to start your iguana on a varied diet as soon as you obtain him.

Get your iguana's eating habits off to a good start by feeding a varied diet right from the beginning.

Omnivore to Herbivore?

There have been reports that as iguanas mature they go from being omnivores to being herbivores. This is an old idea and is controversial.

The latest evidence from observations of iguanas in the wild reveals them to be strictly herbivores all of their lives, from young, newly hatched babies to grizzled old iguanas. In fact, iguanas are called *folivores*—leaf-eating animals.

Previously, it was incorrectly recommended that iguanas be fed either dog food or cat food. There are those who recommend dog or cat food just for hatchlings and then an all-vegetarian diet as the iguana

> ### GET OUT YOUR FOOD PROCESSOR
>
> All food to be given to the iguana, especially if young, must be cut up or shredded. This will promote healthy eating and your pet will avoid choking. Food processors are an invaluable aid to preparing your iguana's meals.

matures. There is possibly some evidence now that this type of diet leads to kidney disease later in life. Therefore, based on the natural habits of iguanas, it is best to feed your iguana only plant material. Also, fruits make up a small portion of the natural diet of iguanas, so fruits should be only about 10 percent of the pet iguana's diet.

Feeding Baby Iguanas

Hatchlings and baby iguanas can be fed the same vegetables as adults. But these young iguanas may benefit from having their food chopped and shredded into small pieces.

Among the things that you can feed your iguana is a commercially prepared food that has the correct ratio of calcium to phosphorous (at least 1.5 to 1).

Fast-Growing Lizards

The hatchling can survive up to three days on its yolk sack. Within three years it will increase its total body weight by 100 times. If it were a human and weighed seven pounds at birth, by age three it would be seven hundred pounds!

Iguanas owe this incredible feat to their digestive system. The iguana's digestive system is very much like that of a cow. It is the bacteria that live in the iguana's and the cow's gastrointestinal systems that help the animal to break down the fiber and high-cellulose materials in their diets.

Because iguanas grow so quickly, they need a sufficient amount of calcium in their diets. Iguanas who lack calcium tend to grow slowly and exhibit metabolic bone disease leading to skeletal problems. It's important to feed the proper ratio of calcium to phosphorous: You want high calcium and low phosphorous in all the foods you offer your pet (the ideal rations are 2:1).

Don't get lazy about feeding your iguana a variety of fresh foods, like collard greens, squash and strawberries.

Commercial Products

There is an ever-increasing number of new iguana pet care products out on the market, especially where food is concerned. As with all food products, you need to read labels carefully. If the food is made from anything other than vegetable material, you should not feed it to your iguana. It would not normally eat that in nature. Then, check out the types of vegetables listed on the ingredients. If there is a lot of cornmeal and other starchy vegetables, this is probably not the best food for your iguana.

In any case, the prepared food should only be a supplement to your iguana's diet; it should not be the only food eaten. Your iguana "is what it eats," and it is truly better off with real vegetables.

If you don't have the time or inclination to feed a 100 percent natural diet, make sure that no more than 15 percent of the overall diet is a commercial mixture. Don't get lazy about feeding these magnificent animals. Imagine if, as an adult, you were still eating baby food!

Vitamins & Minerals

There are a number of vitamin supplements available on the market. Until enough research is performed in regard to iguana nutrition, we will never know the exact requirements for this group of animals. Therefore, it is a good idea to use a commercial vitamin supplement.

Some people suggest making up a large salad for your iguana and then taking a vitamin tablet or vitamin powder and crushing it into small pieces, spreading it throughout the salad. Then mix the salad and feed this to your iguana. Whatever you don't use that day you can freeze for later use. Most pet iguanas will also need extra calcium added to their diet. There are many products on the market for iguanas and even those marketed for people are good for iguanas.

ABOUT LETTUCE

Iguanas love lettuce. However, it must be noted that some types of lettuce are not particularly good for your iguana. Lettuce such as iceberg carries few nutrients and can be called the junk food of the iguana world. Some types of lettuce have no redeeming nutritional value for the iguana. They're like potato chips, nachos or cheese curls. In small doses they're fine, but don't make them a large part of your pet's diet. If your iguana is already addicted, then work hard to change the diet. In the long run, you'll have a much happier, healthier pet!

One word of caution: Use a calcium supplement that does not contain any other ingredients, especially no phosphorus and no vitamin D_3. Phosphorus can bind calcium and should not be in a mineral additive.

There is mounting evidence that vitamin D_3 given by mouth is not effective and possibly may harm iguanas, so don't give a calcium supplement that has it. You can do the same thing with the calcium supplement that you can with the vitamins: Crush a calcium tablet into a salad for your iguana. Make sure to read the labels to ensure you're getting the freshest possible product at the height of its potency.

Feeding Schedules

BABIES

Baby iguanas need to be fed every day, twice a day. For hatchlings a plate of baby food or pureed food should be left out on a flat dish. Make sure they get various vegetables and few fruits. Be sure to alternate food types.

It is extremely important to widen the pallet of the iguana at an early age, and make sure you don't spoil it by feeding it the same food each day. After awhile, it will eat nothing else. You have to expand these animals' taste buds while they're young.

Iguanas can eat everything from apples, bananas and grapes to zucchini, peas and kale. (Keep fruits to 10% of the diet.)

ADULTS

A healthy iguana needs to be fed only every other day.

Water

Make sure there is always fresh water somewhere in a bowl inside the enclosure. As the iguana gets larger, some owners make the bowl larger, as iguanas will want to get wet from time to time. Change the water once a day.

EATING FECES

One of the less colorful aspects of owning an iguana is that it likes to eat feces. Anthropomorphically, it may be a less than ideal habit, but it may have a biological adaptation. Newly hatched iguanas "inoculate" their digestive system by ingesting adult iguana feces, as they need the bacteria to aid in digestion of food. It is not known if older iguanas also need to do this. Infrequently, pet iguanas have been seen eating their own feces. It is unlikely this is a behavior practiced in the wild, because iguanas inhabit such large home ranges that they may not come into contact with one another.

Bananas are tasty treats! But fruit should make up only 10 percent of the iguana's diet.

The Sun Is Food

One way to look at the sun is that it injects nutrients into the iguana's skin—naturally! The effect of the sun is to increase the body's level of vitamin D_3, which increases its level of calcium. Exposure to sun rays is the "magic trick," the best thing you can do for your iguana. Unfortunately, some people still set the iguana by the glass window "in sunlight," failing to understand that the glass is blocking the UV rays.

If you want your iguana to have bones that do not crumble, bend or swell and you want your iguana to live more than a year and be healthy, then you must give him some direct sunlight.

BABY FOODS

Human baby foods are often an excellent resource for the owner who is dealing with a baby iguana who is a difficult eater or an adult who is ill. Stick to the no-preservatives, no-sugar, low-sodium brands. Hatchlings or very young iguanas may need to be force-fed with a dropper for the first few days. Ask your veterinarian to show you how to feed your baby iguana with a dropper.

Dietary Guidelines

The following is a guide by which you should feed your iguana. It lists different groups of nutrients and states what percentage of that group you should feed the iguana. To guarantee optimum health and liveliness, you should vary your pet's diet. It will also affect your iguana's awareness and activity.

GROUP 1: Greens

(25–40% of total volume)

These are leafy greens, including kale, escarole, mustard greens, collard greens, spinach and parsley. In lesser amounts you might try dandelion greens, romaine lettuce and endive.

GROUP 2: Bulk Vegetables

(25–40% of total volume)

This group includes such vegetables as peas, carrots, corn, green beans, lima beans and zucchini. In lesser amounts you might also mix in summer squash, avocado, tofu and okra.

GROUP 3: Fruit

(10% by volume)

Fruits such as pears, peaches, strawberries, oranges, blueberries and cantaloupe are excellent food sources. In lesser amounts you might want to try hucklcbcrrics, raspberries and apples.

GROUP 4: Commercial Foods

(5–10% by volume)

This is a diverse group because of the way that prepared foods are manufactured. Read the labels and be sure that the food you are using does not contain animal material.

chapter 6

Grooming
Your
Iguana

Aside from trimming its claws, there is very little grooming an iguana requires. It may need a daily light misting or bathing, but these are fairly simple procedures.

General Appearance

The healthy iguana's skin should be clean and smooth with a healthy sheen. The skin color may gradually change over time—the key word being *gradually*. Any sudden color variations should be inspected and investigated by your veterinarian at once. In a healthy iguana, the eyes fill the sockets, the animal has a healthy appetite and there should be no bloating or swelling in any of the limbs or belly.

Bathing

Most iguanas love to swim and take a bath. It is easier to start this routine early in life rather than when your iguana is an adult. If you bathe your iguana, make sure that he dries off properly so that he doesn't get chilled.

To bathe your iguana, simply put a large bowl of luke-warm water in the enclosure with the iguana. Hopefully, your iguana will climb right in and do its thing. Do this at least once a week.

The purpose of a good bath is to clean the iguana and loosen up any skin that might be ready to come off, as iguanas do shed their skin (see the sidebar on page 71). Also, this gives your iguana something fun to do! Leave the water in the enclosure for two or three hours, then remove it and leave plenty of time for the iguana to dry off. It's that simple.

You can see the skin shedding on this young iguana. Bathing helps the shedding process.

Some people will put their iguana into the tub to let it swim. This is not recommended because of the possibility that your iguana could shed a bacteria called salmonella in the tub; whoever uses the tub next would be exposed to this bacteria, which can lead to severe illness or even death in humans. Although you can disinfect the tub against salmonella, it is best to always be on the safe side and not let your iguana swim in the tub. (See Chapter 7 for more on salmonella in iguanas.)

Misting

Once a day, spray the iguana's enclosure using water in a small spray bottle with a mist nozzle. Do not aim the mist directly at the iguana. Rather, aim it up, so that it falls like rain or mist onto the enclosure and the iguana. Make sure the spray is as fine as it can be.

This simple practice accomplishes several things. Like a bath, it helps aid in proper shedding. It also provides air humidity. It is thought by many veterinarians that pet iguanas in the home environment do not get enough humidity and are chronically dehydrated. And misting provides water in a form emulating that found in the iguana's natural habitat.

An iguana's skin gets darker with prolonged exposure to sunlight.

Make sure that you do this, like bathing, early in the day, to ensure the evaporation of the water droplets before the lights are shut off. Proper evaporation is a must to misting and bathing. Any moisture left on the skin during the colder hours after the heat lights have been shut off may cause your iguana to get chilled, and this will harm the iguana's health.

If you mist your iguana daily, you must be that much more prepared to clean the enclosure properly. The buildup of moisture in the enclosure can lead to bacterial or fungal growth in the cage, endangering your pet's health. This is especially true if you use an absorbent substrate such as pellets, chips or sand.

Skin Darkening

Sometimes, when iguanas are basking during the day, they begin to turn a darker color, sometimes black. This will only happen for brief periods. It's only when your iguana turns pale or suddenly changes to colors like orange or yellow that you need to worry and seek the help of a qualified veterinarian.

Sneezing

Iguanas posses special organs called nasal salt glands. To empty these glands, they sneeze. When the animal sneezes, it is expelling salt from its passages. This is very healthy. In fact, most people don't see their iguana sneezing, but what they do see is a buildup of salt on the side of the enclosure. That is normal.

Clipping Claws

This is an important grooming technique to master. If not done regularly, your iguana will eventually injure itself, maybe another iguana, and possibly you—all quite unintentionally with nails that are too long. Most manmade enclosures do not provide enough natural abrasive surfaces to wear down the iguana's claws.

In nature, the iguana's claws grow long and sharp and are its best weapons, whether facing another iguana or another species. They can use these claws to help climb trees. These claws can be long, thin, and razor sharp, and do lots of damage. The trimming of claws should be done on a regular basis.

You will need three things to do the job correctly: good restraint, clippers and some kind of clotting agent. Nail clippers for cats or birds will do fine for iguanas and can be purchased at any pet shop. A clotting agent like Kwik Stop or common cornstarch is necessary in case the nail is trimmed too far down and starts to bleed. Restraint depends on your iguana and your ability to hold your pet.

When trimming the nails of any pet, it is important to cut off only the sharp tips. Inside of each nail is a blood

> **SHEDDING**
>
> Iguanas shed their skin. Bathing helps shedding skin loosen up so it can come off more easily. Only when the skin is practically off are you advised to pull off any of the dead skin. It sometimes needs to be gingerly pulled off the dorsal crest. If it does not come off easily, then leave it. Never remove skin prematurely: If the skin doesn't come off easily and if you have to tug hard, then leave it. By prematurely removing skin, you expose your iguana to scarring and a lowering of his immune defenses.

vessel called the quick. The quick extends through the body of the nail, but ends before the tip of the nail. If you cut too much of the nail off, the iguana will most definitely flinch and blood will appear. It is important at that point to rub the coagulant into the nail quickly.

If left open, the wound, especially in an iguana, could lead to serious infection. The bleeding should stop within a minute.

Again, only cut the sharpest end off. If you cut to the quick too often, your iguana will resist handling at any time and you'll end up with a bloody mess every time. And it is painful to the iguana.

The first time it happens you will feel horrible. The animal obviously feels pain and of course you feel bad because you have hurt your pet. Make sure you jump back on the horse, though. If you give up after that, it will take you forever to get back to it. Just do it carefully. And make sure the area is extremely well lighted so that you can see what you are doing.

Two people should be involved in clipping the iguana's nails, one to hold the iguana, the other to clip off the sharp tips.

DOING THE CLIPPING

To properly cut the nails of an iguana there should ideally be two people. Both of you will hold the iguana down as there is one person at the head and throat and the other holding the back legs and the base of the tail.

It is very helpful to wrap the animal in a towel, leaving only the claw to be cut exposed. The iguana seems to feel safer in this situation. It is important to make sure your iguana is calm and you do not fight with it too much. You must remember that grooming is all part of handling.

Hold the iguana's digit in your hand. Especially in young iguanas, the quick will be visible as a thin red or black line running down the inside of the claw. Then, carefully, clip off just the sharpest point, just the tip of the nail.

Its claws are the iguana's best weapons, and will grow long and dangerous if left unclipped.

If you have an emery board, some expert iguana handlers like to give the nail a quick rub with an emery board to file it down. This requires patience and strict attention. Only the very end should be cut off. Some experts feel it's necessary to lightly rub the claws to be cut with rubbing alcohol or hydrogen peroxide to ensure there will be no infections. After a while this will become a fairly simple routine, and will not seem as difficult as it does at first.

There are some iguana experts who recommend that you never cut an iguana's nails. They feel that your pet needs these nails to climb in its enclosure and that as an owner of these magnificent animals, you need to get used to having a pet with claws, just as if you own a dog, you get used to a pet with sharp teeth!

> **FIRST-TIME CLIPPER**
>
> For first-time owners, it may be a good idea to have the first clipping done by someone more familiar with the proper technique. If the iguana associates you with bad grooming experiences, it will avoid you. It is important to learn to do this correctly. The best advice is to have your veterinarian do it the first time and ask if you can watch, so as to learn properly.

What I recommend to owners is to be careful when you clip nails if you have an iguana that especially likes to climb. Your iguana will not realize that you have clipped its nails and as soon as it begins to climb, it will fall. I have seen iguanas break their backs from these types of falls. So clipping is a personal decision and you need to take into account your iguana's habits when you clip nails.

General Maintenance

The enclosure should be cleaned at least weekly, if not more often. The water should be changed daily. If you have an aquarium, empty it out and clean all the sides. Also, replace the substrate and make sure the entire area is clean. An unclean area will wear down the immune system of an otherwise healthy iguana.

If you have carpet or Astroturf on the floor of your enclosure, make sure to clean that, too. If you have an older iguana, you may want to have a sandbox in the enclosure for the iguana to defecate in, as adult iguanas will discharge in the same place consistently.

Iguana Grooming Basics

You wouldn't think so, but grooming your iguana will be a lot like grooming your cat or dog! Here's what you'll need to do regularly:

- Clip nails: Left untended, your iguana's nails will grow long and sharp. Such nails can hurt you or your iguana by tearing skin; they can also get stuck in fabric or wire meshing, causing the iguana to risk injury by struggling to free itself.

- Give a bath: Iguanas love water, and besides taking short swims in their water bowls, should be allowed to swim in a large container of water at least once a week. They also like to be misted.

- Tend to shedding skin: Yes, iguanas shed—just like your furry friends! They shed their skin in pieces, and you may need to help remove these occasionally. You'll certainly need to remove dead skin from the iguana's environment.

- Pay attention to overall condition: Keep an eye on your iguana's skin, noting color and texture.

Recognize what's healthy so you'll know when something's off.

- Keep him clean: Don't let a small problem become a big one by letting general grooming and hygiene slip. Keep your iguana and his cage clean.

chapter 7

Your
Iguana's
Health

The health problems your iguana can develop range from minor to life-threatening. Most require veterinary assistance and some just necessitate an adjustment in husbandry. It is important to be able distinguish the difference between a healthy iguana and one that is ill. Inspect your iguana regularly for signs of good health so you can find the first signs of illness.

The following are conditions you should check for every day.

Appetite　Does the iguana seem active at mealtime? Does it have a healthy appetite or is it not eating?

Behavior　Is your iguana unusually quiet? Does it react normally to its surroundings? Is it reacting to you? Is it sluggish?

Nose　Is there evidence of a discharge around the nose?

Eyes Are they sunken into the sockets? Are they swollen? Is there good eye movement? Are the eyes quick and responsive?

Mouth Is the mouth open? Is the iguana panting? Is there any mucus or foam or any dried crust around the mouth? Is any part of the mouth or throat swollen?

Limbs Are any of the limbs or toes swollen? Are there any toes that have changed color? Is the iguana able to move all of its limbs? Does it walk on all of its limbs? Does it have all of its toes?

Skin Are there any cuts anywhere on the body or limbs? Are there any unusual discolorations or markings on the skin? Are there any open cuts? Is the crest intact?

Sneezing Is your iguana sneezing more than you would expect?

Vent Is the iguana's vent messy? Is the stool firm or loose? Is your iguana having normal bowel movements? Is it straining?

Your iguana should show interest at mealtime and have a healthy appetite.

Finding a Veterinarian

Before you obtain your iguana, it's a very good idea to have a veterinarian already selected. If you have any friends who have iguanas, ask them for recommendations. With the growth in popularity of the iguana, more and more veterinarians are becoming skilled in how to diagnose and treat iguana illnesses. Ask your veterinarian if he or she is a member of the Association of Reptile and Amphibian Veterinarians. This is an organization that informs veterinarians on the latest health information on these types of animals.

It's important that you choose a veterinarian who explains to you in clear, concise language how to take care of your pet. And if your iguana gets sick, you also want your veterinarian to be able to fully explain what is wrong.

Don't be afraid to ask questions and get second opinions. If your veterinarian makes you feel silly every time you ask a question, it's time to get a new veterinarian. As the pet's owner, you are its guardian and you pay the bills, and it's important that your veterinarian have a bedside manner you're comfortable with.

Just as there are many different types of pet owners, there are many different types of veterinarians who differ greatly from one another. Some know much about iguanas and some don't. Find a veterinarian who knows quite a bit. You need to be sure that you have a veterinarian who feels comfortable with iguanas and knows the medicine of these animals well.

In a perfect world, we would all live near veterinarians who are knowledgeable about these pets. But unfortunately, there are almost no courses in veterinary school on iguana medicine. What your veterinarian knows about these pets he or she has learned though reading, attending meetings, experience and dedication. We are not all so fortunate to live in areas where these types of veterinarians practice. What do you do if you don't? You find a veterinarian who you trust and make

---

AN IGUANA GROOMING AND FIRST-AID KIT

It's a good idea to keep a box filled with the necessary materials to care for your iguana. Below is a list of some of the things that would be good to have around.

1. Antibiotic ointment
2. Hydrogen peroxide for cleansing/disinfecting
3. Betadine solution for cleansing/disinfecting
4. Nail clippers
5. Gauze for cuts and wounds
6. Cornstarch to stop minor bleeding

sure that this veterinarian can access the needed reference information on your pet and discuss your pet's health with colleagues.

Health Overview

There are many different types of diseases and illnesses that can affect your iguana. The most common diseases are those caused by improper husbandry and, sadly, these are the most preventable. These problems usually come from one source: inadequate nutrition.

Infectious diseases such as parasitic and bacterial disorders also routinely attack iguanas. Then there are problems like lacerations, nose rubbing abrasions, improper shedding, skin infections and broken tails and limbs, all of which require a visit to your veterinarian.

BURNS

This is one of the most common of external accidents and it is completely preventable. Lizards seek out the warmest thing they can and try to get as near to it as possible. Although heat lamps can be placed safely outside the enclosure, heat rocks, placed inside, are a common source of skin burns. Slight burns may heal themselves, but they will leave scars. Serious burns require immediate veterinary attention. It may take many weeks to months for a burn to properly heal. If not attended to, a burn can be fatal.

LACERATIONS (CUTS)

Lacerations can be caused by a number of objects, including sharp nails or claws; scratches or bites from another iguana; or rubbing against something sharp in the enclosure. These wounds may vary in their seriousness, ranging from abrasions to deep cuts. These need to be addressed immediately. For anything more serious than an abrasion, you need to seek a veterinarian's help. If it is possible to cleanse the wound without harming the iguana and harming yourself, you can use clean water to douse the wound. *Do not use Band-Aids or adhesive strips of any kind.* Deep lacerations are very serious problems, considered emergencies, and need to be seen by a doctor as soon as possible.

NOSE RUBBING

This is one of the most common ailments iguanas suffer, due to poor husbandry and your iguana's need to explore. Iguanas will rub the skin right off of their snouts. If this is not treated quickly and earnestly, it may require surgery and leave your iguana scarred for life. Most of the time it is a result of a cage or enclosure that is too small or too cluttered for the iguana. It can also be a sign that there is inadequate light or heat and the iguana is trying to get to a warmer area.

Iguanas rub their noses against the walls or top of the cage in an effort to escape. If you have a wire cage, you may want to replace it with plastic-coated fine wire mesh, which will reduce rostral abrasions. Make as many changes to the enclosure as necessary, as it is the only long-term cure.

Make sure that when you first notice the swelling and the rawness of the snout, you remove your iguana from the enclosure and make appropriate husbandry changes. Wash the abrasion and coat it with an antibiotic ointment. Change the environment around the enclosure in any way you can to make your pet happier. Treat the snout for a few days, and watch your pet closely. If the wound does not heal within a few days, contact your veterinarian.

Iguanas can cut themselves on sharp edges, so be sure the cage you choose has no exposed wires or unprotected corners.

TOE OR NAIL DISORDERS

Most broken or torn toes or nails are the result of an iguana's getting its claws stuck in something. It will pull and twist until its toe either becomes disjointed, a nail snaps off or it breaks the toe. Of course, people who let their older iguanas have the run of the house are sometimes known to step on their pet's feet accidentally. Most of these injuries need veterinary attention.

BROKEN LIMBS

When a long bone of the leg or arm is broken, it is usually the result of an accident or the first sign of metabolic bone disease. Iguanas are built to take some serious punishment in the wild and are very active, especially when they feel frightened or threatened. Excellent swimmers and runners, they can jump, swim and run at blinding speeds. So, it is unusual for your iguana to break its bones with normal activity. If your iguana fractures one of its limbs without an accident occurring, then the cause of the break is probably a metabolic bone disorder.

Broken bones need to be attended to by a veterinarian as soon as possible. If the break is due to an accident, your veterinarian will recommend a plan of treatment. Probably, radiographs (X rays) will be taken to see how serious the break is. Then your doctor will recommend the best way to treat the break, whether it be confinement, a splint or surgery. Broken bones caused by metabolic bone disease, which results from nutritional deficiency, are treated differently, correction of the husbandry problems being the first priority.

Iguanas given the run of the house are prone to getting their feet stuck in things or of being stepped on (accidentally!) by their owners.

BROKEN TAILS

In nature, the iguana, like other lizards, has some excellent defense mechanisms. One of them involves the tail. When attacked by predators, iguanas are sometimes caught by the tail.

81

All iguanas shed their skin, which can lead to problems if the skin has trouble coming off. You can help by bathing your iguana regularly.

Luckily enough, an iguana's tail is meant to break. There are even special places in the tail bones that are meant to break, if needed, so that when a predator catches the iguana by the tail, the tail breaks loose from the body and the iguana runs away while the predator is left with a tail in its mouth. The appendage will continue to wiggle and writhe, thus holding the attention of the predator while the iguana makes its escape. So if for some reason your iguana loses its tail, do not be upset; the iguana may grow a new tail! If your iguana loses most of its tail, it may not grow all of it back. The shorter the piece of the tail it loses, the better the chances it will all grow back.

Depending on the type of break, there may be no urgency involved regarding seeking medical care. As long as the break occurs on the last third of the tail, little bleeding will occur and regeneration of a new tail will begin almost immediately. If the break happens too near the tail base, then the iguana requires immediate veterinary attention. This is considered a wound and must be cauterized quickly in order to avoid massive bleeding and infection.

Be forewarned: There is little you can do to help in the regeneration of your pet's tail. Many times the tail will grow back thicker and shorter and a different color. Almost always, the second tail will never be as long and thin and whiplike as the first. Some iguanas have even been known to grow a forked tail during regeneration!

IMPROPER SHEDDING

What is improper shedding? As we discussed earlier, sometimes the skin does not come off readily. This is especially true of the skin around the toes. If the skin on a toe becomes wrapped tightly, one end of the toe may become incredibly swollen. If this problem is not addressed, your iguana will probably lose that toe. It is important that when shedding begins you pay extra special attention to your pet's toes. Don't try to peel off skin that isn't ready to come off.

Iguanas shed as they grow and will not shed their entire skin the way most snakes do. Also unlike snakes that shed in one piece, iguanas shed in many pieces. This is normal. The iguana may shed over its back one week and then over its belly the next. This is okay. But in time, all areas of the body should have new skin. If there is an area that never sheds, this needs veterinary attention.

One of the best ways to facilitate shedding is to bathe your iguana at the time shedding is taking place. A bath in lukewarm water will help to soften up the skin and allow it to come off more easily. Also, daily misting will help with a problem shed.

A Word on Salmonella

It is best to assume that your iguana carries in its intestines the bacteria salmonella, which can live there harmlessly or may cause a disease like diarrhea. Even without signs of disease, salmonella can be in the stool of your iguana, and a person who does not practice proper hygiene may ingest some of these salmonella bacteria.

Proper hygiene means never allowing anything that has contacted iguana feces to contact anything that will enter a person's mouth. That means washing your hands whenever you touch your iguana, especially if you are eating or preparing food. If your iguana roams around your house, make sure it does not enter food preparation areas. And if it defecates in the house, make sure you clean it up thoroughly with a cleaning agent such as bleach.

One must be especially vigilant with children and iguanas. Children are always putting thier hands in their mouths, and do not realize the dangers of salmonella.

If your iguana goes in your bathtub, you should make sure the tub is well washed out before a person uses it. It is important to teach children to thoroughly wash their hands after handling their pet iguana.

DIAGNOSING SALMONELLA

It is not easy to diagnose salmonella disease in your iguana. Your veterinarian can do a fecal culture, but even if it is negative for salmonella, your iguana can still be silently harboring salmonella. And if it is positive for salmonella, it does not necessarily mean that salmonella is making your iguana sick.

If *you* have salmonella, you may become sick with diarrhea, dehydration, stomach cramps and/or high fever. You need to see your doctor immediately. If infants or people with suppressed immune systems get salmonella, they can get extremely sick and even die. That is why salmonella is such a serious disease and why strict hygiene should be followed, not just with iguanas but with all reptiles.

Given all of this, one can see why some in the media have been attacking the practice of keeping iguanas as pets. Many of us who work with and keep reptiles feel that these attacks are overblown. There are millions of examples of people who have had reptiles as pets who have never gotten sick with salmonella. Yes, salmonella is a serious disease, but with proper hygiene it is totally preventable. Remember, it is more common to get salmonella from improperly cooked meat or eggs than from your pet iguana.

You may be thinking, *If my iguana has salmonella—which is a bacteria—why can't I have my veterinarian give it antibiotics?* Unfortunately, that won't work. Salmonella is not easily cured with antibiotics, and treating for it may just cause the growth of resistant strains of bacteria.

METABOLIC BONE DISEASE (MBD)

Metabolic bone disease is the most common and preventable disease in iguanas. Most cases of MBD are seen in young iguanas, but it is also seen in female iguanas who are producing eggs but are not being supplemented properly.

Metabolic bone disease is a husbandry problem caused by malnutrition or overall improper care of an iguana. An iguana must have the correct nutrients, plenty of heat and lots of ultraviolet light. An environment lacking in any of these three required components can result in MBD.

This iguana suffered from a calcium deficiency in its diet, which caused the deformity in its backbone.

One of the first signs of MBD in your iguana is found on the face, especially the jaw. It feels rubbery. You can actually squeeze the jaw bone when pinched together. Bones should be strong. The other bones will soon start to be affected, too. First, they may become swollen, almost giving a Popeye appearance to the bones. Actually, the swelling is the body's attempt to compensate for the lack of calcium.

As the disease progresses, bones in this condition are apt to break, including the bones of the spine. The head may become misshapen, as the upper and lower jaws don't come together properly. Sometimes a tail that breaks off too easily is the first sign of MBD. In young iguanas, this results from a diet that does not contain enough calcium, a lack of sunshine or a source of ultraviolet light, a lack of heat or all of the above.

85

Although the causes are simple and easy to identify, the treatment needs to be dealt with professionally. You must seek out a veterinarian immediately. Your veterinarian will probably run a number of tests including examination of a stool sample, blood tests and X rays. Your veterinarian may also give your iguana a number of injections and may force-feed your pet.

Advanced MBD sometimes necessitates intravenous injections. Some veterinarians administer calcitonin to speed recovery. This should never be given to your iguana unless it is under the care of a veterinarian, as incorrect administration will kill your pet.

Your veterinarian should spend a considerable amount of time discussing with you what you need to do to change the conditions that caused this disease. The good news is that the changes caused by MBD are reversible if caught early enough. Many iguanas go on to live a healthy, normal life. If caught too late, the iguana may end up with deformities, especially a broken back, that affect its daily life.

Metabolic bone disease is also seen in female iguanas that have poor husbandry or a marginally good diet. Female iguanas that are producing eggs need extra nutrients to compensate for all that their body requires to produce those eggs. (Remember, a female iguana doesn't need a male around to produce eggs.) When a female has to start using her bone stores of calcium to make eggs, the bones become soft.

If your female iguana starts laying eggs, please contact your veterinarian to make sure that her diet is

HOME CARE FOR THE ILL IGUANA

There are four things you must remember when dealing with an ill or recuperating iguana:

1. Don't handle your iguana at this time. Iguanas find contact stressful. By touching your iguana as a means of consoling it, you will achieve just the opposite effect, as it stresses from the contact.

2. Make sure to raise the temperature of the basking site within the enclosure. Warmth will always help an ailing iguana. Also, maintain a cooling-off place where the iguana can go when it is too hot.

3. Rehydration is very important. Many iguanas become dehydrated when ill. Fine misting and bathing will help your sick iguana.

4. Stay in contact with your veterinarian. This is the most important thing you can do for the health of your iguana.

adequate, especially in terms of calcium, to prevent MBD. It is always much easier to prevent a disease than cure it once it occurs.

KIDNEY DISEASE

Kidney disease in iguanas seems to be more common than it was in the past. The reasons for this remain unknown. It may be due to too much protein when young, being fed animal protein, chronic dehydration or something else we won't discover for a while.

Kidney disease is most common in young to middle-age iguanas (three to five years old) and seems to hit the large, fast-growing iguanas that appear nice and healthy on the outside—that is, until they get sick. Also, many of these fast-growing iguanas are fed animal protein while doing their growing. There have been numerous stories appearing in print of iguanas who have dined their entire lives on canned dog and cat food, macaroni salad and a number of other tasty human foods. Who knows if this is good for them?

If your iguana develops kidney disease, it will become lethargic, stop eating, maybe change color, and lose weight. If you start seeing these signs, take your pet to the veterinarian as soon as possible. The physical examination, blood tests, radiographs and a sonogram may be needed to diagnose this disease.

The only chance to save your iguana is immediate and aggressive treatment. This is a serious disease in iguanas and it is most disturbing, as the iguanas most commonly afflicted are the fast-growing animals whose very attentive owners thought they were helping their pets by giving them foods that would help them grow fast.

Kidney disease sometimes results in gout. It is very rare to have gout without kidney disease. Gout, which is not that common in iguanas, affects the joints and the surface of the internal organs. It causes a white substance called uric acid to be left in the joints or to coat the surface of internal organs like the heart, the kidneys and the liver. Gout will make your iguana feel very sick and can be diagnosed by a veterinarian. By the time kidney disease causes gout, your iguana's kidneys are probably very weak and the chances of recovery are not good.

THE STOOLS

Healthy

The consistency of your iguana's stool will tell you a lot about its health. If the stool is sort of jellylike, with a white, milky finish, you have a healthy iguana. If it's hard and dry, then you have a sick iguana. A healthy iguana is also very regular.

Water is essential to keep your iguana properly hydrated.

The best way to keep your iguana regular is to provide it with a proper diet with lots of vegetable fiber, plenty of water, heat and light. The iguana needs water to hydrate its system. The sun and the heat help the iguana's digestion system function properly.

Iguanas typically have one vent movement per day. Most often they dispose of these wastes in the same place, so as to keep the rest of their living area clean. Most often, they discard their excesses in their water bowl.

Diarrhea

Any number of disorders can cause a temporary case of diarrhea in an iguana. Stress is the most common factor. A change in diets is another main reason. Diarrhea can also be brought on by infections by bacteria, protozoa, nematodes and other parasites.

For the first day or so, try to change your iguana's diet to firm up its stool, supplementing its usual meals with fiber-rich foods. If the diarrhea does not improve after two days of treatment, you will need to consult with your veterinarian. By itself, diarrhea may not seem like a serious medical problem, but it could lead to the loss of water and nutrients that can eventually lead to the death of your pet.

Constipation

Iguanas suffering from constipation may become lethargic. They will appear bloated. Their actions and reactions will be much slower than usual. They may appear to strain and try to defecate but nothing comes out. One cause is a lack of hydration. Without proper amounts of water, the iguana cannot pass its waste and the intestines will become impacted. Another common cause is the lack of proper environmental temperature and the lack of a proper diet.

Iguanas with MBD usually become constipated due to a lack of calcium, which allows the intestines to work properly. Finally, an iguana kept on a dirt or gravel substrate can eat this material, causing a blockage and constipation. Mild cases may respond to water baths. This will usually cause them to pass their waste. Make sure not to put your pet's head under the water.

More serious cases should be brought immediately to your veterinarian. And, remember, you need to correct the conditions that caused this problem in the first place.

ENDOPARASITIC PROBLEMS

These include protozoa, pinworms, roundworms, tapeworms and flukes. Whenever your iguana has diarrhea or a watery stool consistently, one of the above parasites must be considered as a cause. Many iguanas are

routinely dewormed before they are sold. It is important to remember that iguanas depend on some of
these organisms to help them properly digest their
foods. But sometimes these parasites, or others, grow
in too great an amount for your iguana's system to
hold them in check. More often than not, domestically
raised hatchlings suffer fewer cases of infections.
Imported hatchlings or imported iguanas who were
caught in the wild are more prone to many of these
problems.

To detect these organisms, a fecal examination should
be done on your iguana by your veterinarian. If your
iguana has a good appetite, solid bowel movements
and seems healthy and alert, chances are that it does
not have an endoparasitic infection. But an ounce of
prevention is better than a pound of cure, as many
of these parasites, out of control inside their host's
body, may obstruct the intestines or do more serious
damage to the intestinal tract of your pet.

MITES

These are the most common ectoparasitic problems
that confront iguanas. Mites are not always easy to find.
You have to look hard to see them. They live on and off
of your iguana. Sometimes the skin infected with mites
will turn black and blotchy. More than just an annoy-
ance, mites can carry disease. Mites are not so easy to
cure, and sometimes the cure is also harmful to your
pet. There may be many products on the shelf of your
pet store to cure mites, but I would recommend that
you contact your veterinarian before doing anything.
You need to treat both your pet and the area he lives
in. Your veterinarian has safe ways of curing your pet of
this condition.

TICKS

In wild-caught iguanas, ticks sometimes hitch a ride to
your house. They need to be removed as they can carry
disease and debilitate your iguana. Like in other animals, an iguana's ticks need to be removed carefully.
They look like little black and brown seeds attached

to your iguana's body. Sometimes they are small and flat—that's how you know that they are relatively new—and sometimes they are big and roundish, which means they've been feeding for a while.

Make sure to dab the tick with rubbing alcohol and let it sit for just a few minutes before removing it. Then, with a pair of tweezers, gently remove it. The objective with a tick, as always, it to make sure you get the whole tick and not just the body. If you are not sure you can do this, please go see your veterinarian.

RESPIRATORY PROBLEMS

Just like you, the iguana can get a respiratory infection. This usually occurs in stressed iguanas such as those recently imported or those with improper husbandry conditions. How can you tell if your iguana has a respiratory problem? It will act just like you do when you have a cold: It will lose its appetite, sneeze, have a runny nose, and lack energy and may even breathe very hard.

The best thing you can do before you see the veterinarian is to supply plenty of water and make sure you increase the temperature of the hot zone in the enclosure, as this will hopefully strengthen the bodily processes in your iguana. If you live in a relatively cool area, especially the north, damp cold can be an iguana's worst enemy. Make sure you have sufficient heating twenty-four hours a day.

REPRODUCTIVE PROBLEMS

Both the males and the females have reproductive problems that necessitate visits to the veterinarian. The male iguana has two hemipenes, which are part of his reproductive system. Sometimes the male will injure himself and damage either or both of his hemipenes. Sometimes the hemipenes prolapse, meaning they come out of their sac in the area along the tail near the vent and can't be replaced. If not treated swiftly and properly, a problem like this could result in the loss of one of these hemipenes.

Females produce eggs even without the presence of a male iguana and they need to lay their eggs. If they don't have proper nutrients, they won't be able to lay their eggs. Or if they can't find a suitable place to lay, female iguanas will hold their eggs. Since they mostly bury their eggs in warm dirt with enough depth, this is a problem in captivity. So they hold on to them, eventually causing an illness called retained eggs.

The condition of retained eggs is recognized by the fact that your female iguana will develop an enlarged abdomen and become lethargic. Again, though some literature will recommend home remedies and other possible drugs toxic to your iguana to help her to expel the eggs, this is not a course of action that should be attempted. The eggs must be removed by an experienced veterinarian, the sooner the better.

NEUTERING YOUR IGUANA

If you own a dog or cat, you probably have had it neutered. This is best for its health. If you own an iguana, you may wonder if you should have it neutered, too. In female iguanas, spaying them prevents them from becoming egg-bound, which is a medical problem. Female iguanas go through egg production each year, and each time they do they are prone to binding and calcium deficiency. These are serious medical problems that can be totally prevented by removing the ovaries and oviduct (spaying). This procedure should be done by an experienced veterinarian. Most people do not spay their iguana until she has problems associated with egg production.

In males, neutering (removing the testes) is not a common procedure. This is because there is no medical reason to do this. When people want their male iguana neutered, it is for behavioral reasons. As previously stated, male iguanas can be very aggressive towards other iguanas and their owners. A once sweet, easy-to-handle male iguana may turn into a tail-swishing, person-chasing reptile who actually poses a risk to his owners.

Veterinarians have neutered these aggressive males in an attempt to stop this sexually related behavior. Recently, veterinarians have been neutering male iguanas before they become sexually mature to see if this procedure done early in life decreases male sexual aggressiveness. The jury is still out as to whether this is going to be a successful way to curb this problem. As with females, neutering of male iguanas should only be done by a veterinarian experienced in these procedures.

Your Happy, Healthy Iguana

Your Iguana's Name _____

Where You Got Your Iguana _____

Your Iguana's Age (upon purchase) _____

Your Iguana's Diet

    Favorite Foods _____

        Vegetables _____

        Fruits _____

    How Often You Feed _____

Your Iguana's Health

    Name of Veterinarian _____

    Address _____

    Phone Number _____

    Description of Illness _____ Date Noticed _____

        Treatment _____

    Description of Illness _____ Date Noticed _____

        Treatment _____

    Description of Illness _____ Date Noticed _____

        Treatment _____

Your Iguana's Growth (if bought as a baby)

    Size when Purchased _____

    Size Six Months Later _____

    Size One Year Later _____

    Size at Full Growth _____

Favorite Things to Do with Your Iguana

_____

_____

chapter 8

Handling

Your

Iguana

It's important to remember that if you saw an iguana in the wild, it would run away, slither off into the water or do anything else it could to get away from you. It wouldn't come near you for all the juicy green leaves in the world. Iguanas are solitary creatures and they don't even like hanging around with each other, except during mating season.

As discussed in previous chapters, the iguana is a very nervous animal and is very wary of sudden movements, loud noises and busy traffic. Your iguana is not a dog. It will not come when called. It may not even acknowledge your presence except at feeding time. Although they can be very interesting characters once they feel comfortable, these are not hug-me, squeeze-me types of animals.

Like people, iguanas are individuals. Get to know your iguana before you try handling him or her.

All iguanas are individuals, and like human beings, have unique personalities. Some iguanas will become relatively interactive, by iguana standards, and be more than content to be picked up and carted around. Others may not allow you to pick them up, and still others may not react to you one way or the other. However, all these animals have one thing in common—they all require the patience, perseverance and love of an owner who will go slowly and who understands them.

NEVER GRAB AN IGUANA!

You must be very careful when handling an iguana. A tame iguana will be more than happy to climb onto you. Many needless injuries are caused by owners who grab their iguanas by the tail (which often breaks off) or by a limb. This is not the way to approach the handling of an iguana. You could easily injure your pet.

In the Beginning

The first tricks to master are quietness and slow, deliberate movements. You need to build trust. Sudden or fast movements are those of a predator. Someone who moves slowly is probably not interested in eating the iguana, and at least the animal can watch you better, and hopefully feel more comfortable. After it is apparent that the iguana is comfortable, then you can begin interaction.

How do you know when the iguana is comfortable with you? When it stops fleeing when you come in the room, it is comfortable with you. When it stops freezing in place when you are near, it is comfortable with you. When you come to feed it, does it hide, or does it come eagerly toward the food? With an iguana, if it doesn't flee or freeze while you are in its presence, then you are making progress. This painstakingly slow process may take up to two to three weeks or longer. It depends completely on the personality of the iguana, each of which is an individual.

A good way to acclimate your iguana to touch is to feed it by hand. This way it associates your hands with food.

First Touch

When you're ready to attempt to touch the iguana for the first time, remember again that your actions should be slow, deliberate and quiet. A good way to acclimate the iguana to touch is to feed it by hand. This builds trust between you and the animal. When you're going to pick up your iguana, make sure you offer it your hand. Once it knows you, it will, given the proper personality, learn to walk onto your hand.

Iguanas hate being grabbed and picked up roughly. It is the best and fastest way to destroy the trust you built up with the animal. Never attempt to catch your pet by the head. Instead, pet him on the back of the head and on the sides. These first attempts at handling should last no more than 10 to 15 minutes in the beginning of your relationship. And they should be repeated every day.

Eventually you should be able to hold the younger or baby iguana in your hands and let the iguana run back and forth from hand to hand. It may try to escape, but gentle handling and persistence eventually shows the iguana that there is nothing to fear. After several weeks the iguana should seem calmer during these sessions.

When Not to Hold Him

One thing to remember is never to pick up an iguana, especially a male iguana, when he is in his most aggressive posture. This is when he is standing as high up on his legs as he can, with spines erect, and with his mouth open.

DON'T KISS YOUR IGUANA

Neither children nor adults should ever let their lips touch the iguana or put their own fingers into its mouth. Also, owners must always wash their hands after handling their iguana. This is because iguanas can carry salmonella, an infectious bacteria.

The bacteria salmonella is highly contagious and can easily be transmitted from lizards to humans by touching an infected animal and then ingesting the bacteria. Mild cases result in excessive diarrhea and vomiting. Severe cases can even result in death. (See Chapter 7 for more on this.)

If you suspect your male feels threatened—if his dewlap is enlarged or he's hissing or thrashing his tail—don't attempt to handle him.

In responding to what he thinks is a threat, the iguana will expand the dewlap under his mouth and open his mouth, hissing loudly. His tail will definitely twitch Especially if this is an older male, don't even think about handling him. There is the chance, with an older male, that you could get bitten and/or scratched. Come back a little later and see if you can start over.

Holding Your Iguana

It is important that you don't hold an iguana like you would a puppy or a newborn baby. There are two right ways to hold an iguana and a thousand wrong ones. The most important thing in holding an iguana properly is to support the chest and the tail area.

To hold an iguana properly, you need to support the chest and the tail area. These kids are sitting quietly and letting the iguana walk back and forth between them.

Some people will hold the chest from underneath with one hand and the back two legs and tail with the other. The other position is to let the iguana rest along the length of your forearm, carrying the iguana like a football. Either way you are supporting the chest and tail area firmly, without causing undue stress to the animal.

Taking Your Iguana with You

Though many experts do not advise novices to take their iguanas outside without putting them in some kind of sun cage or other portable enclosure, there is a time when you can finally take your iguana out for a walk. You have to be sure, though, that your iguana can handle the experience. Being naturally reserved, solitary creatures, this can be too overwhelming for your pet. You have to train him to accept a harness with a lead or to stay on your arm or shoulder with the harness on while you're out.

This young, outgoing, confident iguana has been trained to walk on a lead in a special harness.

To make sure it will be fun for both you and your pet, start small. If your iguana accepts having the harness on its body, let it wear it around the house. Give it a favorite snack so it associates the harness with something pleasant. If your iguana does not want to wear it, don't force the issue. Put the harness away and try some other time.

As your iguana becomes used to the harness, leave it on for longer periods of time, and start walking alongside the iguana with the harness on it. Again, getting treats for walks on the harness in the house will help make them pleasant experiences for your pet.

SUNLIGHT AGGRESSION

Many iguanas become hyperactive after spending time in direct sunlight. Your iguana will resist being picked up and may run when you approach. Don't take this personally and don't look at it as a step backward. Merely take the iguana back inside and let it calm down. In a number of hours it will be fine.

The Outside World

Make your first excursion one around the yard, then down the street, gradually extending the area you travel and only if your iguana seems comfortable. When you're out, discourage people from reaching out to touch your iguana unless he is well socialized.

Tell them you're getting it used to being outside with you, and that when your iguana is ready, you'll let them touch it.

An important warning to those who take their iguanas outdoors: When your house-bound iguana is taken outside and experiences natural sunlight, its mood may rapidly change. Iguanas, exposed to the sun, can become more energetic and more aggressive. It will be unpleasant for you to have a surly iguana on your shoulder, and it may bite you or someone else. And it may even try to run away if it is not properly restrained.

As your iguana becomes used to the harness, let him wear it around the house before venturing into the outdoors.

If your iguana cannot handle these types of excursions, don't force it to endure these parading gestures. It may cause irreparable damage to the iguana's confidence and your relationship with your pet. Also, if highly stressed like this, the iguana's health could deteriorate, all for the sake of a walk through town or the mall. Don't do it. For those iguanas who are capable of handling such travel, have fun.

If your iguana is comfortable around you and other people, and you start slow and build up steadily, the two of you may enjoy many walks together. Regardless of whether your iguana is able to travel or not, the joys of befriending these animals are many.

chapter 9

Iguanas

in the

World

With the rise in popularity of the iguana, more people want to see these magnificent creatures in their natural habitat. And they want other people to see their iguana. This chapter discusses satisfying either urge, whether you want to travel to see iguanas in the wild, or whether you want to train your iguana to brave the wild world with you.

Seeing Iguanas in the Wild

Though many of the most beautiful iguanas come from Central America, including countries like Mexico, Honduras and Costa Rica, and even Puerto Rico, the Bahamas and other Caribbean islands, the iguana can also be found somewhat closer to home in the United States.

As was previously mentioned, iguanas have been bred and released in places like Florida, which have weather patterns similar to the iguanas' native habitat. And in these places they are thriving. Of course, there have always been Chuckwallas in Texas, New Mexico and Arizona, and they can be found in abundance along canyons and roadsides throughout the Southwest.

Florida and Texas

In these hot states, green iguanas can be found in numerous wetlands and parks, abiding anywhere where there is running water and trees. Water is a life necessity and is usually found where there is also food and protection. The same goes for the trees. Strange as it may seem, many iguanas have been found in the wooded areas around Miami's International Airport and in some of the suburbs surrounding the airport. But generally speaking, the more remote the area is from human beings, the more likely you are to find a number of green iguanas. Iguanas of five and six feet in length have been reported in these areas.

The green iguana can be found in states with hot climates, wetlands and lush vegetation, like Florida.

When you're doing your iguana-watching, move quietly and make sure you pack a pair of binoculars and a camera with a telephoto lens. You are not going to get too close to any of these animals. Before entering private property to see an iguana, ask permission. Trespassing is a serious offense, and you may be prosecuted. Always make sure of where you are and that the owner knows you're there.

The Great Southwest

This is home to America's native-born **Chuckwalla.** Experts disagree about the number of varieties of Chuckwallas that exist, but Chuckwallas generally are black and brick-red in color, and some have cream-colored tails.

The desert iguana is sometimes hard to see in its native habitat because it blends in with the environment so well.

You can find Chuckwallas anywhere in the Southwest where there are creosote plants. Although Chuckwallas tend to eat insects and other prey, they are mainly vegetarians. Rivers or canyons will be home to these large animals.

Ranging all the way from Utah to Nevada, Arizona, New Mexico and Texas, you can find these big chubby characters in abundance. They tend to sit on ledges or other rocks during the day. Make no mistake, though: They will see you long before you see them. Again, you won't ever get too close to them.

With their large bellies, thick, short tails and lack of spines along the back, these are not as interesting-looking as green iguanas. They are desert creatures, whose colorings blend better with the landscape than the green iguana. It is fascinating to see these fat but nimble creatures quickly navigate the arid landscape, using the crevices in rocks to save themselves from predators.

You can find these animals almost anywhere in the Southwest. When you're driving on the roads in these states, all you need to do is to keep a keen eye trained

on the landscape. Once you spot a couple, you'll begin
to pick them out of the landscape immediately.

Texas and Mexico

The **desert iguana** is a common sight in these places,
though it is by far the smallest of the iguana family.
Growing an average of only twelve
to eighteen inches long, this tan
and gray slim lizard is fast and agile.
Like the Chuckwalla, the desert
iguana lacks the large scaly mane
of the green iguana. The desert
iguana inhabits much of the same
territory as the Chuckwalla and
can be found in many of the same
areas.

According to iguana enthusiasts,
the desert iguana is especially plentiful in Imperial and San Diego

> ### CAPTURING WILD IGUANAS
>
> Do not attempt to capture one of
> these animals. Removing them
> from their natural habitat is illegal
> and prosecutable under the law.
> Also, many of these animals, hav-
> ing had the freedom to roam vast
> areas of ground, would make
> unhappy captives. Why take the
> risk, and why make a beautiful,
> wild iguana miserable?

counties. Those large, duned areas sport a variety of
these sleek little lizards darting through the sandy ter-
rain. Unlike the Chuckwalla and the green iguana, the
desert iguana is an accomplished burrow dweller. They
can dig a deep burrow quick enough to enable their
escape from predators.

part three

Beyond
the
Basics

Complete
Listing
of Iguanas

Although the green iguana is the most popular pet of the iguanid family, there are in fact eight genera in this family, each with their own species. These iguanids have very different sizes, types and colorations. They are presented here for the iguana enthusiast.

The descriptions of the family of Iguanidae are taken from various sources, including R. D. and Patricia P. Bartlett's book *Iguanas,* and Frank Slaven's book *Reptiles and Amphibians in Captivity.* (See Chapter 12, "Bibliography," for more information on these and other titles.)

***Amblyrhynchus cristatus*—Galapagos Marine Iguana**   Listed as CITES (Convention on the International Trade of Endangered Species) Appendix I, this is a protected species. The Galapagos marine iguana was described by Charles Darwin on his trip to the Galapagos Islands. This species is at least a foot shorter than the green iguana, growing to a length of about five feet. There are several types of Galapagos marine iguanas, all peculiar to the island they live on. They have a very special diet. Since these lizards eat fresh seaweed and ocean algae, they are a very difficult species to keep in captivity, which is why none are known to be within the United States. They are the only marine lizard in the world, diving in and out of the pounding surf for their diet. They have the ability to do this because of a special gland that secretes the salt out through the nostrils. They are excellent swimmers. While they do display bright red patches during the mating season, they are normally a brown and gray color.

BRACHYLOPHUS SPP

Brachylophus spp—Fiji Iguana   There are actually two species in this genera and they are found on the Fiji and Tonga islands. Both are endangered, which has garnered them a CITES Appendix I rating. There have been encouraging results via protection and captive breeding in Fiji and in the United States, including at the San Diego, Dallas, Fresno and Cincinnati zoos. Fiji iguanas are very small in length and the males rarely average more than two and a half feet in length, including the tail. The females are shorter. They are usually not available to the hobbyist through any legitimate means.

Brachylophus fasciatus—Fiji Banded Iguana This is certainly one of the most beautiful reptiles on earth. The males are colorfully marked with alternating green and light-blue bands. The females are entirely green.

Brachylophus vitiensis—Fiji Crested Iguana This is an animal very similar to the Fiji banded iguana; however, as the name indicates, the crest at the nuchal area (just behind the head) is substantially higher and more pronounced.

CONOLOPHUS SPP

Conolophus spp—Galapagos Land Iguana These are also listed under CITES Appendix I. Unlike the marine iguana, the land iguana stays solely on land, and as is true of many of the Iguanadae family, is an accomplished tree climber. It eats shoots, flowers, fruits, cactus pads and grasshoppers. It may grow up to four feet in length, and females are slightly shorter than males. Listed below are two species of the

Galapagos land iguana, though some experts would argue that *Conolophus pallidus* and *C. subcristatus* are the same species. These lizards are rarely seen outside of their native regions. They tend to be a yellowish-brown color.

***Conolophus subcristatus*—Galapagos Land Iguana** This is the better known of the two species.

***Conolophus pallidus*—Galapagos Land Iguana** This may be the same species as *C. subcristatus*.

Ctenosaura spp

Found from Mexico to Panama and on some Colombian islands, the *Ctenosaura* genera includes nine species. Known as spiny-tailed or black iguanas, they are commonly available, and some of the rarer species are being bred on farms in several countries. Some are affordable even to the beginning hobbyist. Some zoologists do not recognize *Enyliosaurus* species as an iguana, but it is listed for the sake of completeness.

This group, especially as they become adults, tends not to be brightly colored, although there are exceptions. The thing that differentiates them from other iguanas is the spiny tail. The tail is noted for the winding, sharp, raised scales that protrude from it. Mature adults use this tail as a rather intimidating weapon.

Few of the *Ctenosaura* species grow beyond three feet in length and, as is true of other genera, the females tend to be slightly shorter than the males. Many of these lizards are imported, but captive breeding, especially in the United States, is increasing the availability of these species.

***Ctenosaura acanthura*—Spiny-tailed Iguana or Black Iguana** Averaging more than three feet in length, this species is found abundantly along Mexico's Gulf Coast and in some areas of Central America. This species is more terrestrial than arboreal. Some experts believe that this species is closely related to the *C. hemilopha*.

***Ctenosaura bakeri*—Isla de la Bahia Spiny-tailed Iguana**   Hailing from an island off of Honduras, little is known about this extremely rare reptile. No zoo or private collector is known to possess one of these iguanids.

***Ctenosaura (Enyliosaurus) clarki*—Michoacan (Clark's) Dwarf Spiny-tailed Iguana**   Protected by the Mexican government, several specimens are found in zoos and private collections. This species is closely related to *Ctenosaura defensor,* but it is less brightly colored. The average length in males does not exceed one foot and females are slightly smaller.

***Ctenosaura (Enyliosaurus) defensor*—Yucatán Dwarf Spiny-tailed Iguana**   This is another small iguanid. As the name indicates, this animal is found on the Yucatán Peninsula in Mexico. It is plentiful in its natural habitat. This is perhaps the most colorful of the entire *Ctenosaura* genera, with bands of black, blue, red, orange and yellow across its back.

***Ctenosaura hemilopha*—Sonoran Spiny-tailed Iguana**   One of the larger *Ctenosaura,* the Sonoran can grow up to three feet in length, and its spiky tail usually accounts for more than half of that length. They are quite common in the Baja California Sur area and in the northwest region of Mexico. It is darkly colored and has a stocky body shape.

***Ctenosaura oeirhina*—Roatan Island Spiny-tailed Iguana**   Very much like the Isla de la Bahia iguana, this small iguana comes from an isolated island off the coast of Honduras. The movement of these animals is restricted and few are known to exist outside of their natural habitat. Little is known about their natural history.

***Ctenosaura (Enyliosaurus) paleris*—Central American Dwarf Spiny-tailed Iguana**   Sometimes referred to as the Honduran dwarf spiny-tailed iguana, this reptile is quite commonly found in Guatemala and Honduras. They may grow to be a little over a foot in length and the females are somewhat shorter. They are in the collections of several zoos. They are found in semiarid conditions.

***Ctenosaura pectinata*—Mexican Spiny-tailed Iguana**   This is the largest of the *Ctenosaura genera*, measuring up to four feet in length. Recently transplanted to Florida and Texas, this reptile is native to the Pacific Mexican coast. This species is available to the pet trade. The Mexican spiny-tailed iguana is an excellent example of how environmentalists and trade hobbyists can best work together, as many farms have increased the size of this population to the point that this species is now sold in the trade. This iguana's coloring is dark gray with either yellow or white bands. It is seen in many zoological collections including the Indianapolis, Los Angeles and Bronx zoos.

***Ctenosaura (Enyliosaurus) quinquecartinata*— Dwarf Spiny-tailed Iguana or the Club-Tailed Iguana**   This is the largest of the dwarf iguanas, a dubious distinction, as it routinely measures little more than twelve to fifteen inches in length. It is found in southern Mexico and areas of Nicaragua. It has recently become available to the pet trade.

***Ctenosaura similis*—Spiny-tailed Iguana**   This species is very similar to *C. acanthura*, except that although the black iguana ranges from the southwestern United States and northern Mexico, this species ranges from southwestern Mexico all the way to Panama. The colorings tend to be more vivid than other iguanids, with black, green and yellow markings. Averaging more than three feet in length, this species is very healthy and is occasionally available to the pet trade.

Cyclurae

These fourteen species of iguanas are much larger than the common green iguana. There are many variations of this particular group, the largest subset of the iguana family. The species listed under this heading have CITES Appendix I status and are protected by international law. These animals are prohibited from international trade. On the very rare occasion when they are legally offered for sale, they have been bred in captivity by professionals. Although they are extremely handsome lizards, they are also very expensive.

***Cyclura carinata bartschi*—Booby Cay (Bartschi's) Rock Iguana** This is a highly threatened species, and enjoys protection under CITES Appendix II. Among the rarest of iguanas, the Bartletts report that fewer than 300 of these animals are known to exist in a small area known as Booby Cay in the Bahama Islands.

***Cyclura carinata carinata*—Turks Island Iguana or Caicos Island Iguana** Ranging about two feet in length, these reptiles are known to live on Turks Island and Caicos Island off the Bahamas. They look very similar to the rhinoceros iguana, but are smaller. They have a much larger population than the Booby Cay iguana, but are threatened nonetheless.

***Cyclura collei*—Jamaican Rock Iguana** It was thought that this group of iguana was extinct; however, the Bartletts report that this species was rediscovered in 1990. Probably fewer than 100 specimens are alive at this time. They tend to grow about three and a half feet in length and females are slightly shorter than males. There are a few in captivity in Jamaica, but none are known to exist outside of that country.

***Cyclura cornuta cornuta*—Rhinoceros Iguana or Hispaniola Rhinoceros Iguana** This is the most common and largest lizard of the *Cyclura* genera. Some easily become domesticated and accepting of human companionship, but most will not. These iguanas are known for having a nasty bite, so watch out! They are considered fairly intelligent and can even differentiate their owner from other humans. These are very handsome iguanas.

Not only are the males almost four feet in length, but they are very stocky animals, being the heaviest of all the iguana family. Some weigh up to twenty pounds! This iguana gets the name "rhinoceros" from the conical growths on top of its snout, which are more pronounced on females than on males. It is found in zoo collections throughout the world.

Cyclura cornuta onchioppsis—Navassa Islands Rhinoceros Iguana Thought to be extinct, this smaller version of the rhinoceros iguana is native to the small islands off the coast of Haiti.

Cyclura cornuta stejnegeri—Mona Island Rhinoceros Iguana This iguana takes its name from the tiny Puerto Rican island from which it comes. It is thought that fewer than 3000 specimens remain. Few zoos have extant specimens and no private collectors acknowledge possession of this species.

Cyclura cychlura cychlura—Andros Island Rock Iguana This specimen is unique to the Andros Island, a small island in the Bahamas. Even though this species is more plentiful in the wild than many other *cyclura* species, they are still endangered. They range from three to three and a half feet in length. This group is unique as the females grow to approximately the same length as the males.

Cyclura cychlura figginsi—Exuma Island Rock Iguana This iguana is found on the Exuma Cays of the Bahama Islands. The average length is thought to be less than thirty inches. Only about 1,500 of these specimens are thought to exist at this time.

Cyclura cychlura inornata—Allen's Cay Rock Iguana This iguana, though not brightly colored, is actually one of the more interesting of the iguanids. It has dark brownish-grayish coloring except on the head. The head is usually a light gray to white. Another of the Bahama iguanas, it grows to be a little less than three feet in length and is extremely endangered.

Cyclura nubilia caymenensis—Cayman Island Rock Iguana or Little Cayman Rock Iguana This species resembles its close cousin, the Grand Cayman Island rock iguana, in the sense that the males tend to be more docile and slightly shorter than females. They generally grow a little over three feet in length. Less than 1,500 of these animals exist and have CITES Appendix II protection status.

Cyclura nubila lewsi—Grand Cayman Rock Iguana

These are among the most beautiful of all iguanas as they are a lovely shade of aqua-blue. As in all of the *C. nubilia* subspecies, the males tend to be less aggressive than the females. These iguanas are only slightly shorter than the *C. cornuta.* Fewer than 500 of these animals are thought to be alive. Professionals in the Bahamas and the United States have begun breeding these animals in captivity in an attempt to save them from extinction.

Cyclura nubilia nubilia—Cuban Rock Iguana

This is the second most common subspecies of this group. The Cuban rock iguana is the largest of the rhinoceros iguanas, reaching up to five feet in length. This iguana is also being professionally bred and is available to hobbyists. It originates from Cuba but was introduced years ago to Puerto Rico.

Cyclura pinguis—Anegada Island Rock Iguana

This iguana lives on Anegada Island in the British Virgin Islands. The average length is thought to be a little less than four feet long.

Cyclura ricordi—Ricord's Rock Iguana

This iguana is found on the island of Hispaniola. It is the only place in the world where an island supports two distinct species of the same iguana. It is a somewhat shorter version of its island mate.

There are three more *Cyclura* species, all from the Exuma Cays of the Bahama islands. All are extremely threatened and grow to be less than two feet in length. They are the *Cyclura rileyi cristata*—Sandy Cay rock iguana; *Cyclura rileyi nuchallis*—Crooked-Acklins Island rock iguana; and *Cyclura rileyi rileyi*—San Salvador rock iguana.

Dipsosaurus dorsalis

This species, commonly known as the desert iguana, is generally shorter than the popular *Iguana iguana.*

Found mostly in the southwestern United States and Mexico, it is a desert dweller. There are many state laws that prohibit the capture of wild desert iguanas, and most of the ones that are for sale to the common hobbyist are captive-bred by experts.

Iguana iguana This is the most commonly kept house pet in all of the *Iguanidae* family. This group is not in danger according to CITES. Although it is found from as far south as Brazil to as far north as Mexico and areas of the United States, the green iguanas sold as pets are bred on "farms" in Florida and Texas and Central America.

Iguana delicatissima While it is not yet officially a threatened species, this particular animal—the Antillean green iguana—is losing the battle to remain in its natural habitat. Found on several islands off the Lesser Antilles, the Antillean green iguana is slightly smaller in size than the green iguana. The Iguana delicatissima also lacks the large subtympanal scales of the green iguana.

Sauromalus obesus

The Chuckwalla is the most easily identifiable of all iguanae; it looks like a fattened version of *Iguana iguana*. A native of the Southwestern American deserts, the Chuckwalla uses its most recognizable attribute to its advantage in the wild. When confronted by an aggressor, the Chuckwalla climbs into the narrowest of cracks and fattens itself up, lodging itself into the rocks so that it cannot be pulled out. Its large back is also good for soaking up the sun's rays. Its tail also tends to be wider, thicker and shorter than that of its cousins. There are eleven varieties of *Sauromalus:*

Sauromalus ater ater This species is found from northern California to the Gulf of California.

Sauromalus ater klauberi These iguanas are found from Santa Catalina Island down in the Gulf of California.

Sauromalus ater shawi*—Chuckwalla These animals are found from the Isla San Marcos, from the Mexican Gulf of California.

Sauromalus australis This species is from the Baja region.

Sauromalus hispidus This species is generally found on the Isla Angel de la Guarda and a few other islands.

Sauromalus obesus multiforminatus*—Glenn Canyon Chuckwalla This species is generally found along the Colorado River canyon from Utah to Arizona.

Sauromalus obesus obesus*—Western Chuckwalla This species is probably the most common member of the *Sauromalus* family. It is easily found almost anywhere in the southern United States.

Sauromalus obesus townsendi*—Sonoran Desert Chuckwalla This species is generally found in Sonora, Mexico, and a few islands off its coast.

Sauromalus obesus tumidus*—Arizona Chuckwalla Easily found throughout the Arizona and neighboring Mexican countryside.

Sauromalus sleveni*—Chuckwalla This species is from the Islas Carmen, Coronados, and Monserrate. It is extremely rare and very threatened.

Sauromalus varius*—San Esteban Chuckwalla or Painted Chuckwalla This iguana comes from the Islands of San Esteban, Lobos and Pelicanos in the Gulf of California. Measuring more than two feet in length, this is the largest of the Chuckwallas. This species is also endangered.

chapter 11

Glossary
of Iguana
Terms

Albino   Lacking pigment; skin is usually pink; eyes are red.

Ambient temperature   The air temperature of the environment.

Amblyrhynchus cristatus   Scientific name for the Galapagos Marine Iguana, the only marine lizard in the world. It is a protected specie (CITES Appendix I) from the Galapagos Islands and extremely difficult to keep in captivity.

Arboreal   An animal that is tree dwelling.

Articular   Pertaining to a joint.

Biopsy   Removal of tissue for microscopic examination.

Brachylophus   The classification name for the two species of iguanas found on the Fiji and Tonga islands. Rated CITES Appendix I.

Brumation   The reptile or amphibian equivalent of hibernation.

Caudal   Referring to the back half of the body.

CITES This stands for "Convention on the International Trade of Endangered Species," also known as the Washington Treaty. It is an international agreement protecting endangered animals. CITES issues Appendix I and Appendix II ratings; animals listed in Appendix I are in immediate danger of extinction, and there are numerous laws to protect them.

Cloaca The cavity within the vent through which passes the urinary, digestive and reproductive products.

Conolophus The classification name for the two species of *land* iguanas found on the Galapagos Islands. Rated CITES Appendix I.

Cranial Referring to the front half of the body.

Crest A series of raised scales following the length of the spinal cord and down through the length of the tail.

Ctenosaura The classification name for nine species of iguanas found from Mexico to Panama and on some Colombian islands. These are the spiny-tailed or black iguanas commonly available to iguana hobbyists.

Cyclurae The largest subset of the iguana family, with fourteen known species native to the Bahamas, Jamaica, Cuba, Grand Cayman and British Virgin Islands. The iguanas themselves are large, and are known as rhinoceros and rock iguanas. The *cyclura* iguanas have a CITES Appendix I status.

Deposition The depositing or laying of eggs.

Deposition site The site of egg laying.

Dewlap The large flap of skin under the throat of a green iguana.

Dipsosaurus dorsalis Commonly known as the desert iguana, this specie lives in the southwestern United States and in Mexico.

Diurnal Animals which sleep at night and are active during the daylight hours.

Dorsal The length of the area on top of the back along the spine.

Dysecdysis A name for problem shedding.

Ecdysis Shedding.

Femoral pores Pores located underneath the back legs of an iguana that secrete a waxy substance to mark territory.

Fracture planes These are located in the bones of the iguana's tail. They allow the tail to break off without causing serious injury to the iguana, allowing its escape.

Gavage The name for force-feeding your iguana by passing a small tube down its throat.

Genus One of the groupings of classifications, which falls between family and species.

Gravid A pregnant female holding fertilized eggs.

Gular Anything referring to the throat.

Hatchling A newly born iguana; pertaining to the hatching of its egg.

Helithermic Those animals which bask in the sun to regulate their body temperatures.

Hemipenes Male sexual or reproductive organs located near the vent.

Herbivore An animal which lives completely by feeding on vegetation.

Herpetoculture The actual practice of keeping and breeding reptiles.

Herpetology The scientific study of reptiles.

Hypocalcemia When calcium levels are extremely low in the body.

Iguana iguana The classification name for the most popular specie of iguana, the green iguana. Native to locales ranging from Mexico and parts of the US all the way to Brazil, those kept as pets are bred and raised on iguana farms in Florida, Texas and Central America.

Iguanidae Name for the family which includes the species discussed in this book.

Nuchal Usually referring to the back of the neck.

Oviparous Species in which the eggs hatch after laying.

Oviposition Referring to the actual laying or depositing of eggs, which hatch at a much later date.

Parietal eye Located on top of the head, this lens-like sensory organ helps the iguana to gauge the seasons.

Phalanges The bones located in the toes of an iguana.

Poikilotherms Cold-blooded animals whose body temperatures rise and fall with that of their surrounding climate.

Protozoa One-celled organisms that live inside the iguana's digestive tract.

Rostral Refers to the snout, including the nose, nostrils and surrounding areas.

Salmonella A bacteria found in iguanas that can infect humans.

Sauromalus obesus The classification name for the eleven species of iguanas native to the southwestern American desert and commonly called the chuckwalla. Chuckwallas are known for their defense mechanism of crawling between two rocks and fattening themselves up so they can't be pulled out.

Substrate   Materials used to line the floor of an enclosure for the captive animal.

Taxonomy   The formal, scientific stratification of animal and plant life.

Tympanic scale   A large scale on *Iguana iguana*, just below the Tympanum.

Tympanum   The outside eardrum of the iguana.

Vent   Located on the belly of the iguana, just underneath the caudal area. The vent is an opening through which pass the reproductive fluids as well as daily digestive functions.

chapter 12

Bibliography

Books

Bartlett, R. D., and Patricia P. Bartlett. *Iguanas*. Hauppage, NY: Barron's, 1995.

Blair, David. "Green Iguanas: Keeping Them Alive and Healthy," *Reptiles USA 1996 Annual*: 49–62.

Burghardt, G. M., and A. S. Rand, eds. *Iguanas of the World*. Park Ridge, NJ: Noyes, 1982.

Coborn, John. *Caring for Green Iguanas*. Neptune, NJ: TFH, 1994.

———. *Green Iguanas and Other Iguanids*. Neptune, NJ: TFH, 1994.

de Vosjoli, Phillipe. *The Green Iguana Manual*. Lakeside, CA: Advanced Vivarium Systems, 1991.

Frye, Fredrick L., D.V.M. *Reptile Care*. 2 vols. Neptune, NJ: TFH, 1991.

Frye, Fredrick L., D.V.M., and W. Towsend. *Iguanas: A Guide to Their Biology and Captive Care*. Malabar, FL: Krieger, 1993.

Klingenberg, R. *Understanding Reptile Parasites.* Lakeside, CA: Advanced Vivarium Systems, 1991.

Mader, Douglas R. *Reptile Medicine and Surgery.* Philadelphia, PA: W. B. Saunders, 1996.

———. "Reptilian Gout," *Reptiles Magazine,* 1994, 40–46.

Moenich, David R. *Lizards.* Neptune, NJ: TFH, 1990.

Roberts, Mervin F., and Martha D. Roberts. *All About Iguanas.* Neptune, NJ: TFH, 1976.

Samuelson, Phillip, and Margaret A. Wissman, D.V.M. *Green Iguanas: An Owner's Guide.* Mission Viejo, CA: Bowtie Press, 1995.

Wissman, M., and B. Parsons. "Metabolic Bone Disease," *Reptiles Magazine,* 1994.

Magazines

Reptile and Amphibian. RD #3 Box 3709-A, Pottsville, PA 17901. (717) 622-6050.

Reptiles. Fancy Publications, Inc. 3 Burroughs, Irvine, CA 92718. (714) 855-8822.

Reptiles USA (annual). Fancy Publications, Inc. 3 Burroughs, Irvine, CA 92718. (714) 855-8822.

Vivarium. Journal of the American Federation of Herpetoculturists. P.O. Box 300067, Escondido, CA 92030-0067. (619) 747-4948.